1992

Management and Information Systems in Human Services
Implications for the Distribution of Authority and Decision Making

ABOUT THE AUTHOR

Richard K. Caputo, Ph.D., is Assistant Professor and Director, Goldman-Lazarus Center for the Study of Social Work Practice, School of Social Work, University of Pennsylvania, Philadelphia, Pennsylvania 19104. Since 1982, he served as Director, Research and Information Systems; and since 1985, also as Director, Schweppe Research Institute for Social Issues, United Charities of Chicago, 14 East Jackson Boulevard, Chicago, Illinois 60604.

Management and Information Systems in Human Services

Implications for the Distribution of Authority and Decision Making

Richard K. Caputo

The Haworth Press, Inc.
New York • London

Management and Information Systems in Human Services: Implications for the Distribution of Authority and Decision Making is #1 in the Social Work Practice textbook series.

The Haworth Press, Inc., 12 West 32 Street, New York, NY 10001
EUROSPAN/Haworth, 3 Henrietta Street, London WC2E 8LU England

Library of Congress Cataloging-in-Publication Data

Caputo, Richard K.
    Management and information systems in human services.

    Bibliography: p.
    Includes index.
    1. Information storage and retrieval systems — Social Service. 2. Social Work
administration — Decision Making. I. Title.
HV29.2.C37   1988   361.3'068   87-11971
ISBN 0-86656-663-5
ISBN 0-86656-822-0 (pbk.)

DEDICATION

In Memory of My Mother Emily

Contents

Figures and Tables

FIGURES

TABLES

Acknowledgments

I wish to thank A. Gerald Erickson, Armand Lauffer, Jeanne Marsh, Lawrence J. McKeon and Lynn Vogel for their critiques of the early drafts of this manuscript and for their continual support of its development and completion. I am also indebted to Pauline Viverette who typed the manuscript through its many revisions from start to finish.

Introduction

In the last half century, social soothsayers have noted the advent of new, revolutionary managerial, organizational and social arrangements. James Burnham chronicled the transition from a capitalist to a managerial society.[1] Norbert Weiner applied insights gained in computer technology to the study of human communications; and in his examination of the first and second industrial revolutions, he highlighted the concept of "information" in the Cybernetic Age.[2] Jacques Ellul peered into the year 2000 and saw a world-wide totalitarian dictatorship motivated by technological imperative divorced from human agency, will, intentionality and purpose.[3] George Orwell's classic dystopia, *1984*, vivified Ellul's analysis.[4] William Whyte captured the main ideological tenets and behavioral characteristics of corporate clones.[5] Daniel Bell noted the exhaustion of political ideas during the emergence of a service economy.[6] Herbert Muller expanded upon Lewis Mumford's notion of the "neotechnic" phase of industrialization and upon John Kenneth Galbraith's "new industrial state"; "children of Frankenstein" inhabited his "postindustrial" society.[7]

More optimistically, however, Alvin Toffler turned on their heads the likes of Ellul, Whyte, Bell and Muller. In perhaps the best exposition of futurism, Toffler's *Future Shock* pronounced the end of organization man and of technocracy. Toffler spoke of "the modular man" and the coming of organizational "ad-hocracy." Change eclipsed permanency in all aspects of life, from interpersonal relations to organizational structures, from the "triumphant facts of technology" (information) to the "inner images of reality" (knowledge). Toffler dispelled misgivings about negative impacts of perennial change. In his Third Wave civilization, the "fortress of managerial power" is shattered. That pyramidical bastion of managerial experts and super elites who seized the "means of integration" and, with it, "the reins of social, cultural, political, and economic control" was characteristic of Second Wave, industrial society. Toffler's Third Wave extolled new ways of organizing on less hierarchial and more "ad-hoc-ratic" lines, with increased pressures for decentralization of power and for organizational structures more responsive to increased levels of diversity and complexity.[8]

John Naisbett wrote, like Toffler, in an effort to understand the present. In doing so, he provided a roadmap to the 21st century; in *Megatrends*,[9] he identified ten. Most pronounced were shifts from an industrial to an information society, from centralized political, organizational and administrative structures to decentralized ones, and from pyramidical hierarchies to participatory networks. In the information society, information replaces capital as "the" strategic resource: information in the hands of many displaces money as the source of power and a knowledge theory of value eclipses a labor theory of value.

The extent to which the concept of information has come to equal that of technology in the last half century and, perhaps, will surpass it in the next, can be seen in more recently published works by Jeremy Campbell and Alvin Toffler. In *Grammatical Man*, Campbell used information theory to explain and unify the diversity of observations from physics and mathematics to biology and linguistics. Information theory links the symbols, messages and codes of computers and telecommunications to those processes native to living organisms and human knowledge. Like Naisbett and Toffler, Campbell is unequivocally optimistic in his synthesis of seemingly diverse phenomena. The "lesson of information theory" is basically a balance between choice and constraint: as complementary aspects of society, choice and constraint lead not toward oneness or sameness, the way of entropy, but toward the "genuinely new" and the "endlessly complex" products of mind and nature, the way of history.[10]

In *Previews and Premises*, Alvin Toffler confronts the likely impact of the "Information Age" on political and organizational life. In short, issues of "the control of information, privacy, and the management of information flow" become increasingly important. Meta-information becomes the key to control. Power no longer equals knowledge but rather "knowledge about knowledge." Toffler reiterates his forecast that Third Wave society will be more democratic than Second Wave industrial society. He bases this forecast on the diversity and availability of communication channels and devices: tape recorders, paper copiers, cable television and the like. Toffler also argues against the formation of a class of "cognitariats," i.e., a cognizant, united group of coordinators, technicians, knowledge handlers and manipulators. He envisions an expansion or spreading of the "decision load," i.e., those decisions of a certain degree of complexity to be made within a given interval of time, and, concomitantly, to a growth in the percentage of people involved in making those decisions. Finally, Toffler claims computer use makes technically feasible the "demassifying" of society, that participation in decision-making processes that affect society in general and organizations in particular will increase.[11]

Although technology and information have become integral to contemporary life, the sociological phenomenon called "cultural diffusion" leads one to suspect impacts have not been uniformly distributed throughout society. One index of this uneven distribution is the use of the computer, that mechanical device which fuses technology and information into an inseparable whole. In the early 1950s, the Federal government owned most of the computers or contracted with other computer owners, primarily for such applications as defense and nuclear reactor design. By the mid-1950s, there were some 1,000 large-scale computers. This increased to about 30,000 in the 1960s. By 1976, there were about 220,000 computers in the United States and, of these, 40% were considered medium or large computers. These remainder were minicomputers. In addition, there were 750,000 microprocessors. By 1980, there were approximately 750,000 minicomputers and over 10 million microprocessors.[12]

As the number of computers grew, their uses and the kinds of organizations involved in their use broadened, so that by 1980, the major categories of users, by percentage, were: manufacturing industry, 31; miscellaneous business, 13.3; financial institutions, 13.4; wholesale and retail trade, 13.1; educational institutions, 5.7; state and local government, 5.7; and Federal government, 3.4. This left 14.4% scattered about virtually every other kind of organized human activity.[13]

By and large, within these categories, 95% of all computing power is allocated to two kinds of tasks. One is the carrying out of large scale engineering and scientific calculations. The other is the keeping of financial, production and sales records of business firms and other organizations.[14]

More difficult to measure than the distribution of computer usage is the impact of the computer and, with it, of information systems on organizational structure and managerial decision making. Any such undertaking necessitates an inquiry into such concepts as "information systems," "control," types of organizational structures, the nature of evidence, and the like.[15] Much of the work in this area has been done by industry and business. Tom Forester, editor of *The Microelectronics Revolution*, virtually excludes any mention of computer applications outside industry. The attempts to assess the impact of computer technology and information systems are at best rudimentary.[16] Conceptual confusions make any such assessment more difficult.

These difficulties stem, in part, from the fragmentary approach to these analyses and, in part, from the inherent complexity of the phenomena under scrutiny. Although Toffler and Naisbett attempt to synthesize events of contemporary society, their analyses are so broad they fail to provide any useful conceptual framework in which events become more manageable, if not meaningful, in the day-to-day operations of people's lives. At the other extreme, authors of more detailed studies all too readily admit the limitations and restrictions of relying too heavily on empirical analysis, virtually devoid of any theoretical considerations. Thus, on the one hand, grand syntheses add little to the conceptual clarity necessary to more detailed scrutiny and analysis. And, on the other hand, empirical studies fail to integrate organizational theory into the analyses.

These difficulties are compounded further in the human services, particularly in the goals and purposes of organizations. Unlike industry, which seeks profits by producing goods for people, human services, by and large, have the ambiguous task of improving people's lives through the provision of services. Although industry and business and, perhaps to a lesser degree, nonsocial-service service agencies (like libraries), have by and large, welcomed computers, the human services until recently and now only sporadically, have resisted them.

Human service organizations are reluctant, in part, due to the cost of computer systems sufficient to generate the kinds of information managers and professionals are likely to want, but also, in part because there is a lack of knowledge about the benefits to service delivery and professional practice. Although the "microcomputer revolution" may eventually offset the cost factor, there still remains the problem of usefulness.

Beyond routine uses in finance and payroll, and, perhaps, for some data about donors and clients, the problem of usefulness has been addressed only within the past ten years. Much of the focus of usefulness revolves around (1) the use of the computer in human service organizations;[17] (2) the application of computer technology to practice;[18] and (3) a residual potpourri related to information systems,[19] educating professionals,[20] and other miscellany.[21] Much of this literature revolves around the experiences of one agency or organization. Thus, the first 30 years of computer use have already left the human services a score or two behind industry and business and, though to a lesser degree, health and education.

Be as it may, the human services are now faced with the prospect of using microcomputers and becoming part of the "information age." And like business and industry, human service organizations must grapple with the impact of computer and information systems on their organizational structures, their administrative hierarchies and their service delivery. This process of analysis has already begun. Gruber's *Management Systems in the Human Services* and Schoech's *Computer Use in Human Services* are exemplary. Absent from these works, and also from their counterparts in industry and business, is a conceptual orientation to aid our understanding of the meaning of the advent of computer usage not only in particular operations of one agency or setting, but also their mere instrumentality in changing the thoughts of managers and practitioners.

This book rests on the assumptions that information technology is not neutral. Its introduction and implementation create a new environment for decision making, one which alters the patterns of authority and the distribution of the "decision load" within an agency. One most notable aspect of the "information age" is its effect on the distribution of who makes what kinds of decisions in an organization. The position of information specialist or a department of management information systems (MIS) is an example. Historically placed in or under a department that provides support to administration, like accounting or finance, the MIS officer or director increasingly is being elevated to executive level, to influence the direction and policies of the entire organization as well as specific programs.[22]

How the introduction and proliferation of computers and information systems in the human services, as in society at large, industry or business, challenge the daily operations of decision making and service delivery is generally not understood. Computer use and reliance on information systems highlight the importance of rationally and empirically-based deliberations about programs and services. "Information," its nature, availability and use, assumes a central role that helps form questions about the predominant modes of decision making about program and service, namely precedent, practice-wisdom and professional judgment. It also upsets the apple cart of authority, regardless of its institutional or structural legitimacy. And, finally, the role of information and the proliferation of computers place "at risk" not only executives but also direct service professionals, particularly to the extent that they remain accountable for the results and consequences of their services.[23]

Two themes are interwoven throughout the text. The first is that the world view associated with information technology has its own source of legitimating authority. This authority competes against more traditional forms resting on other sources of legitimacy. This book elaborates the operational premises that the distribution of the "decision load" reflects the organizational structure of an agency and that the introduction of an information system in any organization challenges the legitimacy upon which that structure rests.

The other theme interwoven throughout the text is the distinctive nature and management of human service organizations. Contrary to the popular literature arguing for such rationalistic problem-solving strategies as management by objectives in not-for-profit service organizations,[24] attention is given to the loosely coupled nature of most, to the political dimension of decision making, and to the use of supervision to buttress precedent and practice wisdom as the foundations for programmatic and direct-service decisions. On the whole, I contend that an understanding of and an appreciation for computer use and information systems have the potential to alter the bases of power and decision-making authority as they currently exist in an organization. These may be the least disruptive and, perhaps, the most beneficial consequences of introducing computer use into human service agencies.

This book has five chapters. The first discusses three concepts that are the connecting threads to the remaining four chapters. These concepts are authority, decision load and information systems. Here, I am concerned primarily with formal authority and all that that implies in regard to the distribution of functional and programmatic decision making within an organizational structure. The relationship between these three concepts is crucial, because this relationship becomes the central thread, the conceptual link, which connects and unifies the entire book.

In the second chapter, the role of legitimacy in the distribution of the decision load is discussed. The work and critiques of Max Weber, particularly material with a direct bearing on legitimacy are reviewed. A typology of the distribution of functional and programmatic decisions, i.e., the decision load, in light of this discussion of legitimacy and of decision-making theory, is constructed. Finally, there is a discussion of organizational conflicts that invariably arise as professionals seek to maintain their autonomy within bureaucratic structures.

In the third chapter, the nature, structure and management of human service organizations are highlighted. Organizations are examined as "loosely coupled systems," having a turbulent environment of multiple interests and disparate goals with indeterminate technologies and ambiguous criteria for evaluation. In light of these "nonrational" aspects of human service organizations, I discuss the roles of power, authority and control. Finally is a review of the processes of management and decision making in human service organizations.

In the fourth chapter, the development and use of computer technology and information systems in business and in the human services are reviewed. The impact of the development and use of automated information systems on the organizational structure of human service agencies is assessed, as are the ramifications of this development on the authority structure and the decision load.

Finally, in the fifth chapter, information systems is placed in a larger sociocultural and philosophical context. I argue that the proliferation of information technology is one indication of a more global transformation of the way we think about problems and how we act to resolve problems. In my view, technology in general is a 20th century phenomenon whose impact has been viewed in rather negative terms. These views are discussed in the context of man's ability to act intentionally, with self-defined purposes, in the world. A neologism, "technolitics," captures those positive aspects of both technology and politics which enable us to promote decision-making participation within organizational and societal structures.

I hope human services managers and students of administration increase in awareness of the impact information systems have socially and organizationally through use of this work. It is also my hope that this awareness results in the administration of human services that places clients in primacy.

NOTES

1. James Burnham, *The Managerial Revolution* (Bloomington: Indiana University Press, 1960).

2. Norbert Weiner, *The Human Use of Human Beings* (New York: Vintage Books, 1954).

3. Jacques Ellul, *The Technological Society* (New York: Vintage Books, 1964).

4. George Orwell, *1984* (New York: Signet, 1949).

5. William H. Whyte, *The Organization Man* (New York: Simon and Schuster, 1956).

6. Daniel Bell, *The End of Ideology* (New York: The Free Press, 1960).

7. Herbert J. Muller, *The Children of Frankenstein: A Primer on Modern Technology and Human Values* (Bloomington: Indiana University Press, 1970); Lewis Mumford, *Techniques and Civilization* (New York: Harcourt, Brace & World, 1934); and John Kenneth Galbraith, *The New Industrial State* (Boston: 1967).

8. Alvin Toffler, *Future Shock* (New York: Bantam Books, 1970) and *The Third Wave* (New York: Bantam Books, 1980).

9. John Naisbett, *Megatrends* (New York: Warner Books, 1984).

10. Jeremy Campbell, *Grammatical Man: Information, Entropy, Language and Life* (New York: Simon and Schuster, 1982).

11. Alvin Toffler, *Previews and Premises* (New York: William Morrow, 1983).

12. Philip H. Abelson & Allen L. Hammond, "The Electronics Revolution," in Tom Forester (ed.), *The Microelectronics Revolution* (Cambridge: MIT Press, 1980), pp. 16-28.

13. Ibid.

14. Herbert A. Simon, "What Computers Mean for Man and Society," in Forester (ed.), pp. 419-33.

15. Thomas L. Whisler, "The Impact of Information Technology on Organizational Control," in Charles A. Myers (ed.), *The Impact of Computers on Management* (Cambridge: MIT Press, 1967), pp. 16-49.

16. For examples, see William C. House (ed.), *The Impact of Information Technology on Management Operation* (New York: Auerbach, 1971); Rosemary Stewart, *How Computers Affect Management* (New York: Macmillan, 1971) and Thomas L. Whisler, *Information Technology and Organizational Change* (Chicago: University of Chicago Press, 1973).

17. Dick J. Schoech, *Computer Use in Human Services: A Guide to Information Management* (New York: Human Sciences Press, 1982); Lawrence H. Boyd, John H. Hylton & Steven V. Price, "Computers in Social Work Practice: A Review," *Social Work*, 23 (September 1978): 368-71; George Hoshino & Thomas P. McDonald, "Agencies in the Computer Age," *Social Work*, 20 (January 1975): 10-14; David W. Young, "Case Costing in Child Care: A

Critical Step Toward Increased Accountability in Social Services," *Child Welfare*, 52 (May 1973): 299-305; Edwin J. Thomas, Claude L. Walter & Kevin O'Flaherty, "Computer-Assisted Assessment and Modification: Possibilities and Illustrative Data," *Social Service Review*, 48 (June 1974): 170-83; and Gorden R. Wright, "A System of Service Reporting: Its Development and Use," *Child Welfare*, 51 (March 1972): 182-93.

18. *Practice Digest*, 6 (Winter 1983); Paul Abels, "Can Computers Do Social Work?" *Social Work*, 17 (September 1972): 5-11; and Theron K. Fuller, "Computer Utility in Social Work," *Social Casework*, 51 (December 1970): 606-11.

19. Jack H. Donahue et al., "The Social Service Information System," *Child Welfare*, 53 (April 1974): 243-55; David Fanshel, "Computerized Information Systems and Foster Care," in Murray L. Gruber (ed.), *Management Systems in the Human Services* (Philadelphia: Temple University Press, 1981); and John H. Noble, "Protecting the Public's Privacy in Computerized Health and Welfare Information Systems," *Social Work*, 16 (January 1971): 35-41.

20. Paula S. Nurius & Elizabeth Mutschler, "Use of Computer-Assisted Information Processing in Social Work Practice," *Journal of Education for Social Work*, 20 (Winter 1984): 83-94; and Claire M. Anderson, "Information Systems for Social Welfare: Educational Imperatives," *Journal of Education for Social Work*, 11 (Fall 1975): 16-21.

21. Ann M. Rothschild & Jean E. Bedger, "A Regional CHILDATA System Can Work: An Exchange of Letters," *Child Welfare*, 53 (January 1974): 51-57; and Young, "Case Costing in Child Care."

22. Donald W. Kroeber & Hugh J. Watson, "Is There a Best MIS Department Location?" *Information Management*, 2 (October 1979): 165-73.

23. Felice Perlmutter, *Executives At Risk: Management in the Human Services* (Lexington, MA: Lexington Press, 1984).

24. For example, see Peter Drucker, "What Results Should You Expect? A User's Guide to MBO," in Gruber, *Management in the Human Services*.

Chapter 1

Authority, Decision Load and Information Systems: Three Concepts in Search of Their Meaning

This chapter introduces three central concepts: authority, decision load and information systems. Each is treated separately for purposes of clarity only. Nonetheless, significant aspects of each concept are integrated. For example, the concept of information systems draws upon aspects of hierarchy, a part of a discussion of authority in organizations, and of functional and programmatic distribution of decisions, basic to the concept of decision load. The impact of different configurations of authority, the various distributions of decisions, the different uses of information systems in organizational structures are assessed in subsequent chapters. The material presented here is primarily conceptual and descriptive in nature, meant to lay a foundation upon which subsequent chapters build and refine.

THE CONCEPT OF AUTHORITY

Development and Uses of the Idea

The concept of authority is, at best evasive, though much examined. The ubiquity of this concept provides a pool of empirical data for social science researchers: authority in the family; informal authority or leadership in small groups; organizational and bureaucratic authority in such intermediate organizations as churches, armies, industrial and governmental bureaucracies; and political authority in society-wide or inclusive organizations ranging from tribal societies, the modern nation-state and international organizations. Nonetheless, the concept of authority defies a commonly used definition.[1]

Social scientists and political theorists, such as Michels,[2] Etzioni,[3] Friedrich,[4] DeJouvenal[5] and Benn[6] are only a few with distinct definitions of authority. Nonetheless, some common factors of authority can be distilled. One is the notion of legitimacy. Subordinates feel obliged to obey and superiors sense a right to issue commands. Another involves hierarchical roles, like those of parent-child, employer-employee, supervisor-supervisee. Authority relations can be institutionalized to the extent that duties and obligations are specified, behavior is reasonably predictable and relations continue over time. And, finally, authority is a resource available to incumbents of formal positions, carrying with it the possibility of tapping greater and greater resources.[7] By and large, however, the concept of authority continues to receive conflicting treatment and remains a focus of much contemporary attention.[8]

Toward a Working Definition of Authority in the Context of Organizations

In organizational theory, there is wide and varied meaning of authority.[9] Major theorists differentiate the concepts of authority, power and influence. Some, like Peter Blau, contrast authority and leadership.[10] Distinguishing authority from the other concepts are the notions of legitimacy and dependency, particularly in light of cultural vis-à-vis social authority.[11]

By and large, authority signifies the possession of some quality or claim compelling obedience, deference or trust. It invariably implies the suspension of private judgment and the regulation of some action. Social authority describes the high probability that people will obey a command recognized as legitimate according to prevailing rules in society. Cultural authority, however, refers to the probability that particular definitions of reality and judgments of meaning and value will prevail as valid and true. Social authority involves the control of action through the giving of commands; cultural authority is defined as the construction of reality through definitions of fact and value.[12]

Both social and cultural authority involve legitimacy and dependency. Contemporary professionals, for example, derive their authority from four distinctive claims of legitimacy: first, that their knowledge and competency have been validated by a community of peers; second, that this consensually validated knowledge and competence rest on rational, scientific grounds; third, that professionals' judgment and advice are oriented toward a set of substantive values, such as health and welfare; and fourth, that the profession, like authority itself, is anchored in and buttressed by the community-at-large, i.e., by society.[13] Contemporary society has witnessed and nurtured a proliferation of experts who, by their very nature, increase interdependence at best, but who also foster an unwelcomed dependency. Claims for legitimacy and authority go beyond professional competency. Watt, for example, has identified seven types of authority, with equally compelling claims to legitimacy, whose exercise necessitates suspension of private judgment, a regulation of some action or a combination of the two.[14]

The suspension of judgment and the regulation of action are inextricably linked to the related concepts of influence and power. In this regard, Bachrach and Lawler define authority as power based on rights of control and concomitant obligations to obey. They distinguish authority, a dichotomous variable, from influence, a continuous variable. In an organization, one either does or does not have authority to make a particular decision. Someone, however, can have some influence on the decision. Authority resembles a zero-sum game; influence does not.[15]

Authority is also distinguished from influence in its sources and bases of power. It is based solely on formal, structural sources, whereas influence can be grounded in personality, expertise and opportunity (informal structure). The primary bases of power are coercion, remuneration, norms and knowledge. Essentially, the coercive base entails the control of punishment; the remunerative, that of rewards; the normative, that of symbols; and the knowledge base, that of information.[16] All four are bases of authority.

In a given organization, the formal structure may limit one or more power bases, but, on a general level, authority implies all four bases. Superiors typically control rewards or punishments; their prerogatives are normatively sanctioned by the organization's rules; and their formal positions ordinarily give them exclusive knowledge over which they have substantive control. Influence, on the other hand, when its source of power resides in either personality or expertise, has its bases in norms and knowledge, whereas when its source is opportunity, coercion and knowledge form its base.[17]

Another important distinction between authority and influence is the degree to which power is limited. Authority is circumscribed power, since it is lodged in the formal structure of an organization. Its domain (the number of individuals or units under a superior) and scope (the range of activities, responsibilities or behavior controlled for each unit) are typically well specified and formally defined. With influence, neither domain nor scope is specific and clear. Both have a greater ambiguity and variance over time.

Legitimacy is a third dimension used to determine the degree to which power is circumscribed.[18] Briefly, legitimacy implies a belief in the appropriateness of an authority structure. Judgments about that appropriateness might be based on moral values, normative ideals or pragmatic criteria. In any case, legitimacy implies subordinates accept both the authority of a superior and the rationale or justification, whether implicit or explicit for attaching authority to certain positions and their occupants. Legitimacy means subordinates stay within the confines of the existing hierarchical structure and all members of the organization, regardless of their level in the hierarchy, are willing to follow standard procedures for conducting organizational activities. The greater the legitimacy attributed to the structure by organizational members, the greater the compliance an organization can command from its members. And, since authority implies the right to make the final decision, legitimacy refers specifically to beliefs about rights of decision making.[19]

Some Concluding Remarks About Authority

By and large, the issue of authority has a mixed reputation. The young attack it and the aged want respect for it. Parents might have lost it and police seek to enforce it. Experts claim it and artists shun it. Scholars seek it and lawyers cite it. Philosophers reconcile it with liberty and theologians conciliate it with conscience. Bureaucrats pretend they have it and politicians wish they did. And, many say that there is less of it now than there used to be. Authority, for certain, is not of one piece.[20] Nonetheless, it is inextricably linked to unity in common action.

As Simon notes, the most essential function of authority is to issue and carry out rules expressing the requirements of common good.[21] A group of people coming at a common good which can be attained only through a common action must be united in its action by some steady principle. Authority embodies this principle.[22] It, however, transcends rules of methods, for these, invariably, are shaped by the character of the problems they are designed to solve. Authority rests upon the ability of the human will to find commonly accepted and agreed upon actions to achieve common ends. This will, shared in community, is prior to any specific rules of method.[23]

Authority depends upon standards of right and on cultural values that imbue power with morality. It is so imbedded in the organizational fabric of society that people occupying certain positions can issue a message describing the steps necessary for racial integration and others will receive and act on it without further question.[24]

Contemporary society circumscribes the range of subject matters over which an authority has dominion. Ordinarily, authoritative messages are accepted only within a given range of subject matters. This range, the area of obedience or compliance, has been called the zone of acceptance or indifference.[25] In question is the change in this zone prompted by introducing information systems and computer technology into the day-to-day operations of and decision making in human service organizations. Before delving into the relationship between authority and information systems, however, the concept of decision load must be understood.

THE CONCEPT OF DECISION LOAD

Use of the Idea

In its broadest sense, decision load refers to the degree of decision making required to run any society—a certain number of decisions of a certain degree of complexity to be made within a given interval of time. Alvin Toffler, for example, notes that the arrival of industrialism radically increased society's decision load. As Second Wave industrial society eclipsed the First Wave agricultural order, it brought with it a much greater need for coordination and integration, which required many more decisions and decisions about different kinds of phenomena than before.[26]

In preindustrial societies, the number of political and administrative decisions required to keep things running was small. The decision load was minimal. A tiny, semi-educated, unspecialized elite could rule. With expanded trade, an increase in the division of labor and more complexity in society, Second Wave industrial society had a kind of "decision implosion" that also accompanies contemporary Third Wave society. Even more complex and diverse than industrial society, the heterogeneity of contemporary society necessitates even higher levels of information exchange. Advancements in technology, like microcomputers and cable television, permit more varied symbols and messages to flow through society, which, in turn, encourage greater social diversity. And, diversity raises the level of information needed for social coordination and integration.[27]

Toffler highlighted the formative influence of the speed of change itself on society,[28] a corollary of Ogburn's theory of cultural lag.[29] The latter described how social stresses arise from the uneven rates of change in various sectors of society. Toffler's future shock posits a need for balance, not merely between sectors, but between the rapid pace of the environment change and the limited pace of human response. Future shock results from the increasing lag between the two.[30] An aspect of future shock, is what Toffler calls a decisional implosion.

By and large, Toffler defines this decisional implosion in political and governmental incompetencies. There are simply too many decisions to be made too quickly about too many strange and unfamiliar problems. The White House, for example, is responsible for decisions about everything from air pollution, hospital costs and nuclear power to the elimination of hazardous toys. The executive agencies are virtually crushed under a mounting decision load. The number of applications, for example, to the U. S. National Endowment of the Arts has far exceeded its ability to make quality decisions.[31]

Linked to the decisional implosion is the information explosion, demonstrated by the plethora of new communication channels and the new tools for handling data — word processors, optical scanners, microfilm storage and the like. The Second Wave industrial preoccupation with making things shifts to a concern for managing things. Issues of the control of information, privacy, the management of information flow become increasingly important, in politics as well as in organizations.[32]

Toward a Working Definition of Decision Load in Organizations

Nothing in organizational theory envelops the concept of decision load. Like societies in general, organizational structures indicate how decisions requisite to their day-to-day functioning are distributed throughout. Within organizations, it can be said that a certain number of decisions of a certain degree of complexity are made within a given interval of time. The organizational structure, as represented by its organizational chart in its conceptual form at least and in its functional form at best, illustrates not only the "chain of command" and areas of responsibilities, but also the distribution of decisions along lines of programmatic responsibilities. At the very least, the decision load encompasses all those decisions necessary to carry out those programmatic responsibilities. This is far too simplistic, however, because it equates all types and complexities of decisions, no matter at what organizational level.

The decision-making hierarchy describes an organization's structure in terms of the kinds and amounts of information staff need to plan, coordinate and carry out their work. Usually represented by a pyramid with three levels, decision making is stratified into strategic at the top, tactical in the middle and operational on the bottom.[33] A more complete depiction would provide four levels of decision making; these are likely to occur in an organization as a whole as well as in each programmatic component. Figure 1.1 illustrates this four-tiered hierarchy.

Strategic planning is the name for those processes of deciding on organizational objectives, on resources used to obtain these objectives and on the policies which govern the acquisition, use and disposition of these resources. Management control refers to those processes by which managers assure resources are obtained and used effectively and efficiently to accomplish organizational objectives. Operational control applies to those processes of assuring specific tasks are carried out effectively and efficiently. And, operations refers to the actual carrying out of basic activities, i.e., of providing the services requisite to achieving organizational goals.[34] One can view the decision load within an organization as a distribution of decisions among these four levels.

Herbert Simon offers a supplementary breakdown of decision making.[35] He distinguishes programmed from nonprogrammed types of decisions. Decisions are programmable to the extent they are routine and repetitive and specific processes for handling them have been devised. Decisions are nonprogrammed to the extent they are novel, ill-structured and unusually consequential and consequently are better handled by general problem-solving

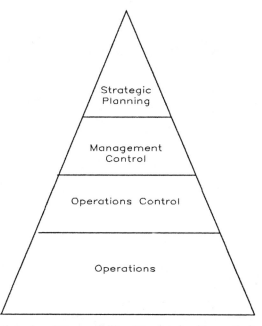

Figure 1.1: Hierarchy of Responsibility. (Reprinted, with permission of the publisher, from *Managing Management Information Systems* by Philip Ein-Dor and Eli Segev [Lexington, MA: Lexington Books, D. C. Heath, Copyright 1978, D. C. Heath & Co.], p. 5.)

processes.[36] Determination of the size of a decision load can be made by examining the distribution of decisions among those in an organization with responsibility for the bulk of nonprogrammable versus programmable decisions.

Ein-Dor and Segev also offer a helpful perspective by superimposing Simon's hierarchy of programmable and nonprogrammable decisions onto the hierarchy of responsibility illustrated in Figure 1.1. Figure 1.2 illustrates this superimposition. The two lower levels of the hierarchy of responsibility, namely, operations control and operations, correspond to programmed decisions and the top two levels to unprogrammed decisions. But, the demarcations are illustrative. No clear-cut boundaries exist, nor does staff exclusively make one type of decision or another. At

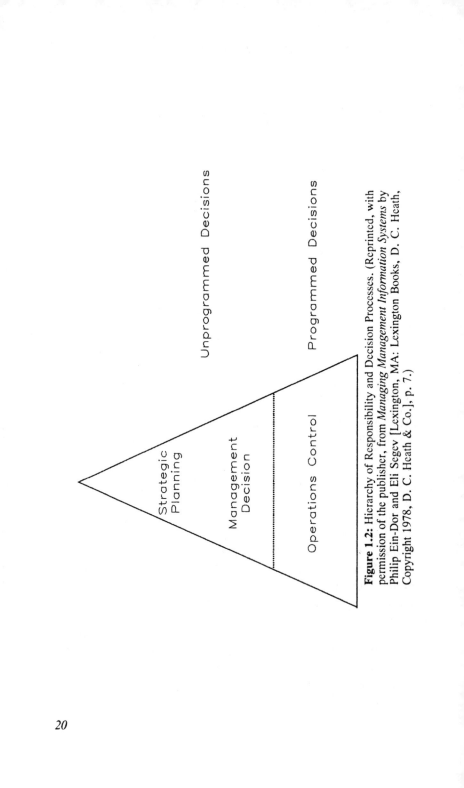

Figure 1.2: Hierarchy of Responsibility and Decision Processes. (Reprinted, with permission of the publisher, from *Managing Management Information Systems* by Philip Ein-Dor and Eli Segev [Lexington, MA: Lexington Books, D. C. Heath, Copyright 1978, D. C. Heath & Co.], p. 7.)

this point, the most we can say is that as the degree of programmed decisions decreases and that of the heuristic-intuitive content increases, the higher the level in the hierarchy of responsibility.[37]

This depiction assumes that people in various positions within an organization make decisions. Whether managers, professionals, semiprofessionals, clerical or manual workers, all make decisions. It is limited to the extent it fails to account for the responsibility for and importance of decisions to others. Nonetheless, it provides a necessary base for formulating a working definition for the concept of decision load. More detail requires a distribution of decisions along lines of both a hierarchy of responsibility and the degree of programmability.

One final approach to developing a working definition of decision load entails an examination of problem areas commonly faced by organizations, particularly human service agencies. Illustrative is a compilation of such problem areas completed by a group of voluntary family and child-serving agencies called IMPAC SYSTEMS, INC. It produced a report which contained an itemization and analysis of agency-based information problems.[38] Some forty or so problems were discussed as decisions to be made to resolve them. There were four subcategories, constituting 77% of all problems stated by member agencies. The main categories were: (1) agency-based problems, (2) problems about an externally generated information base (12%), (3) those regarding external reporting requirements (3%) and (4) those of general research (8%). The four subcategories of agency-based problems included planning (13%), implementation (28%), evaluation (9%) and analysis and research and agency data base (27%). Figure 1.3 is a partial enumeration of major agency decision areas.

To the extent a decision load can be viewed as the burden of decision making required to run an organization, the distribution of that load can be shown to be concentrated in the areas of decision in Figure 1.3. In each area, a certain number of decisions of a certain degree of complexity must be made within a given interval of time.

Figure 1.3.

Major Agency Areas of Decision Making

1. Program planning--Supply and Demand Considerations.

    a. Assessing need.

    b. Planning services to meet need.

2. Program implementation.

    a. Direct services.

        (1) Selection and assignment of clients.

        (2) Scheduling.

        (3) Selection and delivery of service method.

    b. Personnel inventory.

        (1) Inventory of staff resources.

        (2) Inventory of Board resources.

    c. Performance expectations.

        (1) Expectations for direct service staff.

        (2) Expectations for supporting staff.

        (3) Expectations for Board members.

    d. Selection, retention and termination of personnel.

    e. Staff development.

    f. Pricing services.

    g. Procedures.

        (1) Procedures in general.

        (2) Administrative and clerical procedures.

        (3) Procedures involving practitioners.

        (4) Accounting procedures.

        (5) Communication procedures.

    h. Location of decision-making.

    i. Organizational structure.

    j. Facilities--planning and management.

    k. Public relations.

    l. Consumer development.

    m. Funding.

Figure 1.3. (Continued)

Major Agency Areas of Decision Making

3. Evaluation.

    a. Effectiveness.

        (1) Areas of effectiveness.

        (2) Measuring effectiveness.

    b. Costs.

        (1) Cost accounting system.

        (2) Budgeting system.

4. Analysis and research.

    a. Technological problems.

    b. Areas of analysis.

    (1) Community needs.

    (2) Supply considerations.

    (3) Direct services.

    (4) Personnel.

    (5) Staff development.

    (6) Policies and procedures.

    (7) Facilities.

    (8) Public relations.

    (9) Fund-raising.

Source: Adapted from A Master Plan for Information Systems to Serve Local IMPAC Member Agencies (New York: IMPAC Systems, Inc.), 1971, p. I-20.

Some Concluding Remarks About the Concept of Decision Load

Unlike the hierarchy of responsibility and degree of program-mability, areas of decision partially account for the responsibility for and importance of decisions to others in an organization. This is most obvious in Figure 1.3, under the category of "program implementation." Although defined separately, direct services, personnel inventory and performance expectations, for example, are interrelated, if not interdependent, functions expressed in organizational structures and programs. Decisions in one function both influence and are influenced by decisions in the other functional areas. Services dictate the broad parameters of personnel requirement and the personnel department establishes minimum job requirements and screens specific applicants.

Areas of decision constitute the final component of a working definition of the concept of decision load. The hierarchy of responsibility, degree of programmability and areas of decision make up the decision load. The distribution of the number and kind of decisions within an organization can be examined using these three concepts. Such an examination will show the distribution of the decision load is related in part to the distribution of authority and the needs for information in an organization. The nature of these relationships will be examined in subsequent chapters. To enlighten that discussion, the concept of information systems must be analyzed so we may better understand the influence of information systems on decision making and authority in human service organizations.

THE CONCEPT OF INFORMATION SYSTEMS

Use of the Concept

In its most modern sense, the concept of information systems is invariably linked with the development of the computer. This history spans, for all practical purposes, a mere 30 or 40 years. On the whole, however, it is used more precisely than either authority or decision load. Essentially, information is data processed and meaningful to a user. A system is a set of components operating together to achieve a common purpose. These are the hub of organizational information systems, particularly systems for management, our main concern, though we will focus on the use of information to users other than managers, notably, practitioners in a subsequent chapter.

An information system comprises all the people, hardware, software, data and procedures necessary to collect, transmit, process and store data, as they retrieve and distribute information throughout an organization. This information supports operational and managerial functions of an organization.[39] All organizations and agencies have some type of network of formal and informal information flow. Data can be collected, processed and disseminated manually, by machine or in a combination of the two. File cabinets are hardware in one sort of information system. Budgets and case records are information system documents as well.[40]

Implicit in the term information system is the notion of flow. Information moves from one person to another, creating a constant need for decisions, which, in themselves, represent additional information. Because it flows through a decision network, it causes work to be done. In the management context, information flows to an administrator, triggering a decision which, in turn, flows from the manager to the rest of the organization.[41]

Information System Functions

A variety of classification systems help define the functions of a management information system (MIS).[42] The conventional approach matches organizational functions with information-systems functions. Four functional levels of information-system requirements parallel the hierarchy of responsibility presented above: operations, operations control, middle management and top management. In operations, information is concerned with such matters as client identification, service delivery, resource utilization and payments. Operations control includes such functions as identifying and tracking clients, documenting service and worker activities, generating scheduled reports and responding to routine inquiries about amount, types and costs of services delivered.

Information systems also function for middle-management. These derive, for the most part, from middle management re-

142,459

sponsibilities such as monitoring reports on timeliness of service delivery after clients' initial contact with the agency; compliance with performance standards; work-load distribution, client dispositions and outcomes; "tracking" client referrals; and miscellaneous "demand reports."

MIS functions provide information for top management as well. Here, information requirements involve organizational goals, planning objectives, legal actions, responses to legislation, new regulations and other demands on the organization to carry out or modify its functions, since top managers must make decisions about resources used to attain these goals and about policies to govern their use. Typical information requests of top managers (and of funding sources) are: number of people served, outcomes, average costs and likely impact of changes in funding levels.[43] Table 1.1 summarizes those management functions related to specific managerial levels.

Designing the Information System

The design of information systems has been conceptualized in a variety of ways.[44] These boil down to the following prescriptions: determine if a new or modified information system is economically and technically feasible; analyze the existing flow of information, design a working system, including people, tasks, output, procedures and forms; test the system, correct errors and convert the old system to the new one; and, finally, evaluate the new system to determine omissions, commissions or other deficiencies.[45] The steps, procedures, and choices involved in installing an information system are far too many to be covered here. They are best left to technical primers.[46]

There are, however, two aspects of information systems which warrant consideration here: the way the data items are set up or the structure of the data base and its relation to types of decisions it is meant to support. Although the structure of the data base may seem to be a technical matter, in a much larger sense it is more a question of organization design than the MIS itself. There

Table 1.1.

Management Functions at the Various Managerial Levels

| Management Function | Strategic Planning | Managerial Levels | |
		Management Control	Operational Control
Planning	Long range	Medium range	Short range
Organizing	General framework	Departmental level	Small unit level
Staffing	Key persons	Medium level personnel	Operational manpower
Directing	General and long-range directives	Tactics and procedures	Daily and routine activities
Controlling	Aggregate level	Periodic control and exceptions	Regular and continuous supervision

Source: From Niv Ahituv and Seev Neumann,
Principles of Information Systems for Management
(DuBuque, Iowa: Wm. C. Brown Company Publishers, 1982),
p. 123.

are basically two approaches to structuring the data base: the "applications" approach and the "data-base management system" (DBMS) approach.

In the first, each "application," i.e., as payroll, bookkeeping or client data, is self-contained and the computer file for each application file is the responsibility and property of the originating department. In many multiservice organizations, even those stressing collaborative efforts, client data are more likely to be organized by program with little, if any, exchange of records across departments. This reinforces a decentralized agency structure. In the DBMS approach, common data program are pooled and data files are linked or mapped, so data for any program can be easily retrieved by any user and by management. The DBMS approach tends to move the organization toward greater centralization. To moderate either extreme — decentralization or centralization — the two approaches can be combined. [47]

As noted previously, two basic types of decisions are structured ones and unstructured ones. To these we can add semi-structured decisions, i.e., those in which some of the steps in the process are structured and others are unstructured. The component of the organizational information system which provides information for decision makers is called the MIS. It serves the main classes of management actions: first, the system makes structured decisions and, second, it supports the process of making unstructured or semi-structured decisions by performing some phases of the process and providing supporting information for other phases. [48] In the first, for example, a computer program can process inventory transactions and automatically reorder replenishments. In the latter, computer programs can report cost overruns and calculate the impact of various predetermined alternative solutions. [49]

There are two components of MIS logic: structured decision systems and decision support systems. Although these names do not necessarily correspond to conventional information systems, they nonetheless describe the ways in which computer-generated information can be so applied to decision makers. [50] A structured decision system (SDS) supports decisions at the operational and operations control levels of the hierarchy of responsibility. The decision support system (DSS) supports decisions at the management control and strategic planning levels. Table 1.2 summarizes essential characteristics that distinguish these two logical components of the MIS.

Clearly, DSS characteristics, associated with the functions of strategic planning, are diametrically opposed to those of SDS, associated with functions of management control. Decision makers with different levels of hierarchical responsibility make different types of decisions. These are based on different kinds of information, collected, organized and presented in different ways, for different uses.[51] Figure 1.4 is an illustration of hierarchical levels of responsibility, where varying degrees of programmed decisions and different kinds of information and information systems are used. In general, the higher the level in an organization, the less programmed the decision-making process and the more highly processed the information required for making decisions.[52]

Some Concluding Remarks About Information Systems

Attention to information as a key variable in understanding organizations is a relatively recent development. Nonetheless, the differences between structured and unstructured decisions, routine and nonroutine information, structured decision systems and decision support systems and the like are important because critical information is increasingly nonroutine in modern organizations in general and in human service organizations in particular.[53] In light of contemporary demands for increased accountability and sound management, information system development and computerized data base use are inextricably associated with the human services trends to quantify services, to focus on program outcomes, to push for service integration and to encourage planning and evaluation.[54]

These trends, however, both influence and are influenced by

Table 1.2.

Characteristics of SDS and DSS

Attribute	SDS	DSS
A. The User/Decision Maker.		
1. Decision-maker's environment (internal and external)	Constant, steady Relatively simple	Changing, dynamic, complex
2. Decision-maker's level	Operational control	Strategic planning
3. System development initiative	Pushed to decision maker	Comes from decision
4. Decision-maker's involvement in system development and use	Passive	Active
5. Decision-making style	Predetermined, universal, impersonal	Individual, personal, subjective
B. The Decisions Supported by the System.		
1. Structuredness	Structured	Unstructured
2. Time-horizon orientation	Historical, past-oriented	Future-oriented
3. Routineness of use	Routine	Ad hoc, unique
4. Decision-making process	Well defined, algorithmic	Heuristic, iterative, exploratory
5. Importance to the organization	Local, operational	Strategic, organization-wide
6. Decision process phase supported	All phases	Some phases

Table 1.2 (continued)

Characteristics of SDS and DSS

Attribute	SDS	DSS
C. The Information System.		
1. Data sources	Largely internal	Largely external
2. Design predetermination	Structured	Unstructured
3. Data base	Well defined, narrow, detailed, specific	Data redundancy, broad, integrated, aggregated
4. Model base	Predetermined models, quantitative, universal, O.R., explicit	Tailor-made, model building blocks, qualitative, heuristic, implicit, exploratory
5. System design orientation	Data oriented	Decision (model)-oriented
6. Operating mode	Likely batch	Interactive
7. System success criteria	Robustness, operational efficiency	Flexibility, adaptability
8. Frequency of use	Predetermined	Undefined frequency

Source: From Niv Ahituv and Seev Neumann, Principles of Information Systems for Management (Dubuque, Iowa: Wm. C. Brown Company Publishers, 1982), pp. 141-42.

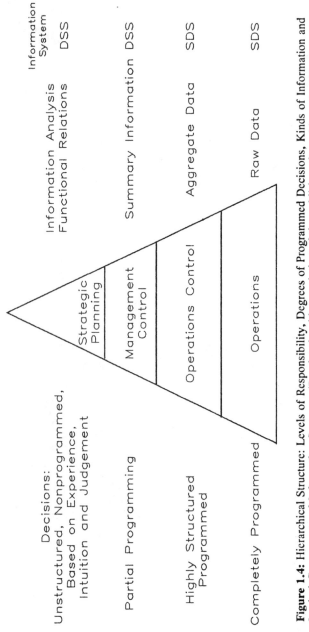

Figure 1.4: Hierarchical Structure: Levels of Responsibility, Degrees of Programmed Decisions, Kinds of Information and Logical Components of Information Systems. (Reprinted, with permission of the publisher, from *Managing Management Information Systems* by Philip Ein-Dor and Eli Segev [Lexington, MA: Lexington Books, D. C. Heath, Copyright 1978, D. C. Heath & Co.], p. 8.)

the way an information system is implemented in an organization. Information enters, more or less frequently, into decision making, and information systems influence the ways this may happen. Information systems, therefore, influence the structure of authority and the number of decision makers and kinds of decisions made in organizations. The introduction of information systems casts a shadow on the sources of legitimacy, of authority, and of power within organizations, and we should explore a redistribution of the decision load in an organization to understand these effects.

SUMMARY

The three major concepts which undergird the entire book are authority, decision load and information systems. A working definition of authority entails possession of a quality or claim which compels obedience, deference or trust. It implies suspending private judgment and regulating some action. Authority involves both the control of action through giving commands and the construction of reality through defining fact and value. Integral to authority is legitimacy, a belief in the appropriateness of authority. Legitimacy implies that subordinates accept both the authority of a superior and the rationale or justification for attaching authority to certain positions and their occupants. Finally, authority is linked to bringing about unity through common action. Ordinarily, the domain of that authority is a circumscribed zone of acceptance or indifference in which authoritative communications are accepted without further question.

The second concept, decision load, relates the hierarchy of responsibility (as indicated by organizational structure and chart) to the degree of programmability (extent of routineness) of decisions and the content areas of decision. Figures 1.1-1.3 illustrate this relationship. Essentially, the hierarchy of responsibility is strategic planning, management control, operations control and operations. The most routine or programmable decisions occur at the operations control and operations levels. Strategic planning and management decisions are the least programmed types of decisions. Major content areas include program planning, program implementation and evaluation. The distribution of the number and kind of decisions made in an organization can be examined using one or more of the three forms of analysis. Thus, the decision load encompasses the number of decisions of varying degrees of complexity (programmability) made by individuals with varying degrees of authority within a given interval of time.

The third concept, information systems, describes information produced to support operational and managerial functions of an organization. Information requirements vary by managerial level as illustrated in Table 1.1. Basically, two components of MIS logic highlight the ways computer-generated information can be supplied to decision makers. SDS support decisions at the operations and operation control levels and DSS support decisions at the management control and strategic planning levels. In general, the higher the level in an organization, the less programmed is the decision-making process and the more highly processed is the information required for making decisions. Differences between structured and unstructured decisions, routine and nonroutine information, structured decision systems and decision support systems are important because critical information is increasingly nonroutine in modern organizations in general and in human service organizations in particular. Information systems influence both the structure of authority and the number of decision makers and the kinds of decisions made in organizations.

NOTES

1. Robert L. Peabody, "Authority," *International Encyclopedia of the Social Sciences*, I, 473.

2. Roberto Michels, "Authority," *Encyclopedia of the Social Sciences*, II, 319.

3. Amatai Etzioni, *The Active Society: A Theory of Societal and Political Processes* (New York: The Free Press, 1968), p. 360.

4. Carl J. Friedrich, "Authority, Reason and Discretion," in Friedrich (ed.), *Authority*, Nomas I (Cambridge, MA: Harvard University Press, 1958), p. 35.

5. Bertrand DeJouvenel, "Authority: The Efficient Imperative," in Friedrich (ed.), ibid., p. 160.

6. Stanley I. Benn, "Authority," *The Encyclopedia of Philosophy*, I and II, 215-18.

7. Peabody, "Authority," 473-74.

8. See, for example, Sebastian DeGrazia, "What Authority is Not," *American Political Science Review*, 53 (June, 1959): 321-331; John H. Schaar, "Legitimacy in the Modern State," in Philip Green & Sanford Levinson (eds.), *Power and Community: Dissenting Essays in Political Science* (New York: Pantheon, 1970), p. 276; Robert Nisbet, *The Twilight of Authority* (New York: Oxford University Press, 1975); Christopher Lasch, *The Culture of Narcissism: American Life in an Age of Diminishing Expectations* (New York: Warner Books, 1979) and *Haven in a Heartless World: The Family Besieged* (New York: Basic Books, 1979); Richard Sennett, *Authority* (New York: Vintage Books, 1970); Daniel Bell, *The Cultural Contradictions of Capitalism* (New York: Basic Books, 1976), pp. 263-64n; and John P. Diggins & Mark E. Kann, *The Problem of Authority in America* (Philadelphia: Temple University Press, 1981).

9. Robert L. Peabody, *Organizational Authority: Superior-Subordinate Relationships in Three Public Service Organizations* (New York: Atherton Press, 1964), p. 5n.

10. Peter M. Blau, *The Dynamics of Bureaucracy: A Study of Interpersonal Relationships in Two Government Agencies* (revised ed.; Chicago: University of Chicago Press, 1964), pp. 223-24.

11. Paul Starr, *The Social Transformation of American Medicine: The Rise of a Sovereign Profession and the Making of a Vast Industry* (New York: Basic Books, n.d., circa 1982), pp. 9-17.

12. Ibid., p. 13; Talcott Parsons, "Authority, Legitimation, and Political Action," in Friedrich (ed.), *Authority*, pp. 197-221.

13. Starr, op. cit, p. 15; Clark E. Cochran, "Authority and Community: The Contributions of Carl Friedrich, Yves R. Simon, and Michael Polanyi," *American Political Science Review*, 71 (June, 1977), 546-58.

14. E. D. Watt, *Authority* (New York: St. Martin's Press, 1982). These types include de facto authority, moral authority, religious authority, rightful authority, civil authority, authority based on rules and reasons and authority based on knowledge.

15. Samuel B. Bacharach & Edward J. Lawler, *Power and Politics in Organizations: The Social Psychology of Conflict, Coalitions and Bargaining* (San Francisco: Jossey-Bass, 1980), pp. 30-31.

16. Ibid., p. 34.

17. Ibid., pp. 36-37.

18. Ibid., pp. 37-38.

19. Ibid., p. 39.

20. John H. Schaar, "Legitimacy in the Modern State," in Philip Green & Sanford Levinson (eds.), *Power and Community: Dissenting Essays in Political Science* (New York: Vintage Books, 1970), p. 276.

21. Yves Simon, *A General Theory of Authority* (Notre Dame: University of Notre Dame Press, 1980), p. 57.

22. Yves Simon, *Nature and Functions of Authority* (Milwaukee: Marquette University Press, 1940), pp. 17-18.

23. Kenneth D. Benne, *A Conception of Authority: An Introductory Study* (New York: Columbia University, 1943), p. 173; Cochran, "Authority and Community."

24. David Easton, *A Theoretical Approach to Authority* (Stanford: Stanford University, Department of Economics, 1955), p. 53.

25. Ibid., p. 54; Herbert A. Simon, *Administrative Behavior* (2nd ed.; New York: Macmillan, 1961), p. 12; and Chester I. Barnard, *The Functions of the Executive* (Cambridge, MA: Harvard University Press, 1938), pp. 168-69.

26. Alvin Toffler, *Previews and Premises* (New York: William Morrow, 1983), pp. 116-17.

27. Ibid., p. 107.

28. Alvin Toffler, *Future Shock* (New York: Bantam Books, 1970).

29. William F. Ogburn, *On Culture and Social Change: Selected Papers* (Chicago: University of Chicago Press, 1964).

30. Toffler, *Future Shock*, pp. 3-4.

31. Alvin Toffler, *The Third Wave* (New York: Bantam Books, 1980), p. 411.

32. Toffler, *Previews and Premises*, pp. 108-09.

33. Linda Dreyer, *Preparing for System Improvement*, Vol. I: *MIS Perspectives* (Portland: Regional Research Institute affiliated with the School of Social Work at Portland State University, 1979), pp. 30-31.

34. For a fuller discussion of these definitions, see Robert N. Anthony, *Planning and Control Systems: A Framework for Analysis* (Boston: Division of Research, Graduate School of Business Administration, Harvard University, 1965). See also, Phillip Ein-Dor & Eli Segev, *Managing Management Information Systems* (Lexington, MA: Lexington Books, 1978), pp. 3-9.

35. Herbert Simon, *The New Science of Management Decision* (rev. ed.; Englewood Cliffs, NJ; Prentice Hall, 1977), pp. 39-81.

36. Ibid., pp. 46-48.

37. Ein-Dor & Segev, *Managing Management Information Systems*, pp. 5-7.

38. *A Master Plan for Information Systems to Serve Local IMPAC Member Agencies* (New York: IMPAC Systems, Inc., 1971). Although IMPAC, Inc.

no longer exists, William B. McCurdy, its former president, is currently the senior vice president of Family Service America. He provided me with a copy of the *Master Plan*.

39. Niv Ahituv & Seev Neumann, *Principles of Information Systems for Management* (Dubuque, IA: Wm. C. Brown, 1982), p. 5.

40. Murray L. Gruber, Richard K. Caputo & Thomas Meenaghan, "Information Management," in *Human Services at Risk: Administrative Strategies for Survival*, ed. by Felice Davidson Perlmutter (Lexington, MA: Lexington Books, 1984), p. 129.

41. R. L. Martino, *Management Information Systems* (Wayne, PA: Management Development Institute Publications, 1969), pp. 26-27.

42. Much of what follows appears in Gruber, Caputo & Meenaghan, "Information Management," pp. 131-34.

43. Project Share, *Planning and Implementing Social Service Information Systems: A Guide for Management and User* (Human Services Monograph No. 25, September, 1981, Aspen Systems Corp.), pp. 37-39.

44. John A. Patton & M. S. D'huyvette, *Automated Management Information Systems for Mental Health Agencies: A Planning and Acquisition Guide*, DHHS Publication No. ADM80-797 (Washington, DC: Government Printing Office, 1980); Dick J. Schoech, Lawrence L. Schkade & Raymond Sanchez Mayers, "Strategies for Information System Development," *Administration in Social Work*, 5 (Fall/Winter, 1981): 11-26; Michael I. Youchah, "An Introduction to Systems Analysis, Design and Implementation," in Murray L. Gruber (ed.), *Management Systems in the Human Services* (Philadelphia: Temple University Press, 1981); and Ahituv & Neumann, *Principles of Information Systems for Managers*.

45. Gruber, Caputo & Meenaghan, "Information Management," p. 132.

46. For example, see Ahituv & Neumann, *Principles of Information Systems for Managers*; Martino, *Management Information Systems*; Project Share, *Planning and Implementing Social Service Information Systems*; and *MIS Perspectives*, Vols. I and II.

47. Gruber, Caputo & Meenaghan, "Information Management," pp. 133-34.

48. See Dick Schoech, *Computer Use in Human Services: A Guide to Information Management* (New York: Human Sciences Press, 1982), pp. 113-27, for a summary of decision-making theory and processes. For an original treatment of the decision-making process, see Simon, *The New Science of Management Decision*, pp. 39-81. See also Peter G. W. Keen & Michael S. Scott Morton, *Decision Support Systems: An Organizational Perspective* (Reading, MA: Addison-Wesley, 1978), pp. 61-78.

49. Ahituv & Neumann, *Principles of Information Systems for Managers*, pp. 138-39.

50. For a series of monographs that address the influence of computers and

information systems on managerial decision making, see William C. Hause (ed.), *The Impact of Information Technology on Management Operations* (Princeton: Auerbach, 1971), pp. 231-310.

51. Ahituv & Neumann, *Principles of Information Systems for Managers*, pp. 140-44.

52. Ein-Dor & Segev, *Managing Management Information Systems*, pp. 7-9.

53. Kenneth E. Knight & Reuben R. McDaniel, *Organizations: An Information Systems Perspective* (Belmont, CA: Wadsworth, 1979), p. 121.

54. Schoech, *Computer Use in Human Services*, pp. 42-59.

Chapter 2

The Role of Legitimacy in the Distribution of the Decision Load

In this chapter the role legitimacy plays in organizational structure and the distribution of the "decision load" is discussed. Too frequently, management students and professionals focus on the pathological aspects of bureaucracy, completely disregarding concern for legitimacy. Since the "information age" challenges legitimacy of authority and power within organizations, attention to these as classically expressed is essential to an appreciation of modern approaches to the study of bureaucracy and to the distribution of the "decision load." This chapter, therefore, summarizes the development of those aspects of organizational theory, namely of authority and legitimacy, made vulnerable by the use of information systems. A typology for the legitimate distribution of the "decision load" of an organization based on modern organizational theories is presented. Finally, there is a discussion of the tensions the typology might generate among professionals, administrators and other experts in human service agencies.

ORGANIZATIONAL THEORY AND THE CONCEPT OF LEGITIMACY

The Contributions of Max Weber

Unlike the history of management thought tracing ideas to Sumerian script (circa 5,000 B.C.),[1] the "classical" approach to the study of bureaucracy and organizations begins in the late nineteenth and early twentieth centuries with Max Weber, who may be regarded as the founder of the systematic study of bureaucracy.[2] His analysis remains one of the focuses of general sociology.[3] Of central concern here is the importance Weber gave to legitimation and its administrative apparatus.

Weber distinguished three principles of legitimacy, each corresponding to a type of administrative apparatus and each defining an "ideal" or pure type of domination.[4] Claims to legitimacy may be based on rational, traditional or charismatic principles. The last are exhibited as devotion to an individual person of exceptional, sanctified, heroic or exemplary character, and of the normative patterns or orders he/she ordains. "Traditional" grounds for legitimacy rest on an established belief in the sanctity of traditions and of those exercising authority under them. The first, "rational" grounds, rests on a belief in the legality of enacted rules and the authority under such rules to issue commands.[5] Belief in legality means the compliance with formally correct enactments, which have been imposed by an accustomed procedure.[6]

In legal or "rational" authority, obedience is owed to a legally established, impersonal order and extends to the persons exercising the authority of office under it, only within the scope of authority of the office. In regard to traditional authority, obedience is owed to that person occupying the traditionally sanctioned position of authority who is bound by tradition. This obligation of obedience is a matter of personal loyalty within accustomed obligations. Finally, the charismatically qualified leader is obeyed by virtue of others' trust in his revelation, heroism or exemplary qualities, so far as these fall within the scope of the individual's belief in his power.[7]

Of primary concern here is legitimacy associated with legal authority or the "imperative co-ordination" of the actions of a group of people. Organizing others requires a relatively high probability that a definite, reliable group of persons will be primarily oriented to executing of leadership's general policy and specific commands.[8] The effectiveness of legal authority is measured by acceptance of the validity of a body of abstract rules and in positions or offices of authority.[9]

Rational legal authority has the following characteristics: (1) a unitary organization of official functions within a set of rules; (2) a specified sphere of activity or competence which involves (a) obligations to perform functions marked off as a part of a systematic division of labor, (b) provision to the incumbent of the necessary authority to carry out these functions and (c) the means of compulsion are clearly defined and their use is subject to definite conditions . . . ; (3) the organization of offices follows the principle of hierarchy; that is, each lower office is under the control and supervision of a higher one . . . ; (4) the rules regulating the conduct of an office may be either technical rules, i.e., prescribed courses of action or norms; and (5) administrative acts, decisions and rules are formulated and recorded in writing. . . .[10]

In the Weberian view, the most efficient and pure manner in which to exercise legal authority is to employ a bureaucratic administrative staff. In this construct, individuals appointed under the highest authority are (1) personally free, subject to authority only with respect to their impersonal official obligations; (2) organized in a clearly defined hierarchy of office; and (3) selected on the basis of technical qualifications. In addition, each office has a clearly defined sphere of competence, is treated as the sole, or at the least the primary, occupation of the incumbent; and constitutes a career.[11]

These criteria, categories and ideas constituted Weber's ideal type of bureaucratic administration called legal-rational. He posited that this type of administrative organization was capable of attaining the highest degree of efficiency and, as such, it would be the most rational means of carrying out imperative control. He deemed it superior to any other form in precision, stability, the stringency of discipline, and in reliability. He concluded "development of the modern form of the organization of corporate groups in all fields is nothing less than identical with the development and continual spread of bureaucratic administration. . . . For the needs of mass administration today, it is completely indispensable."[12]

Legal-rational type of bureaucratic administration's superiority rests on its source of legitimacy: the legality of enacted rules and the right of those elevated to authority under such rules to issue commands. Further, superiority may be accorded it, according to Weber, because it allows an expanded role for technical knowledge. Weber equated bureaucratic administration with an exercise of control on the basis of knowledge. This knowledge includes technical information and skills, by themselves sufficient to ensure a position of extraordinary power, as well as the knowledge that grows out of experience in the service or on the job.[13]

Concomitantly, above all other forms of organization, bureaucratization offers the optimum possibility of specializing administrative functions according to purely objective considerations, minimizing arbitrariness in decision making. Objective discharge of business is done according to calculable rules, without regard for persons, which implies a leveling of status and a "calculability" of results. Paradoxically, these enhance the status of experts, those functionaries with specialized training who, by constant practice, increase their expertise.[14]

It is difficult to summarize Weber's contribution to the concepts of authority, legitimacy and bureaucracy. For our present purposes, a sufficient comment is that, for Weber, authority or the capacity to evoke compliance in others in a bureaucracy, is made legitimate by a belief in correctness of the rules and loyalty to an impersonal order or superior position, not to the position holder. An administration is more or less bureaucratic not from the number of levels of hierarchy[15] or the size of the span of control,[16] rather, the decisive criterion is whether or not the authority relations have a precise and impersonal character, as a result of rational rules.[17]

Refinements of Max Weber's Contributions

Over the years, organizational theorists and social scientists have scrutinized the works of Max Weber, with particular attention to his use of "ideal types." This is a review and summary of a selective representation of those works with a direct bearing on: (1) how administrators and managers, as well as organizational theorists and social scientists think about authority and legitimacy in the context of modern organizational structure and behavior; and (2) how the development and implementation of management information systems affects this thinking, with particular regard to the process and delegation of decision making in organizations.

Weber does not distinguish between organization and administration, probably because he formulated his concept of bureaucracy in his political sociology or description of governmental apparatus. In modern literature, the term bureaucracy refers at times to the administrative apparatus of an organization and at other times to the organization as a whole.[18]

Talcott Parsons attacked this problem distinguishing three levels or subsystems in the hierarchical structure of every organization. These are the technical, the managerial and the institutional. The first are all those activities which contribute directly to the performance of the organization's goals. The managerial subsystem oversees the internal affairs of the organization and mediates between the technical subsystem and its environment through procurement of resources, including clients or customers. The institutional subsystem links the technical and managerial subsystems to the larger society. Each has different functions to perform and, consequently, different structural arrangements for coping with its respective problems. As a result, there is a qualitative break in the simple continuity of line or hierarchical authority Weber postulated.[19]

Weber's definition of authority has also come under extensive scrutiny. As Herbert Simon concluded in 1957[20] and as indicated here in Chapter 1, there is no consensual definition in the literature. Peter Blau, for instance, poses several relevant questions. He notes that Weber's description of authority implies a kind of voluntary imperative control. To answer the question, "How can compliance be imperative if it is voluntary," he suggests the existence of structural constraints rooted in the collectivity of subordinates rather than in instruments of power or in influences wielded by the superior himself. Thus, compliance with a superior's directives becomes part of the normative behavior of the group of subordinates. Voluntary social action is never devoid of social constraints. The compliance of subordinates in authority relationships is as voluntary as our custom of wearing clothes.[21]

In a bureaucratic setting, however, a somewhat broader notion of compliance than the restrictive one in Weber's legal-rational forms the basis of legitimacy. Managerial responsibilities require more influence over subordinates than those designated as legal obligations. Although employees are under contractual obligation to follow managerial directives, the scope of formal authority with its source in a legal contract is somewhat circumscribed. Management's legal authority to assign tasks to subordinates is rarely questioned, but this does not encourage willingness to work hard or exercise initiative. Managers seek alternatives to expand the sphere of compliance with their directives.[22]

Under this broader notion of legitimacy, authority is not a static, immutable quality that people have and others do not; rather, it is defined by consensus.[23] Experimental evidence supports the conclusion that one's perceptions of the authority enjoyed by others as well as by oneself is a crucial variable in organizations.[24] In addition, Barnard notes that authority can rarely be imposed from above, but becomes viable only through the acceptance of those exposed to it.[25]

Legitimation is the process by which authority is accepted by a specific group. This process varies with social (organizational) context[26] and along lines of specific conditions within the group.[27] Description of the variations is complicated by the values of the observer[28] and by the ways management attempts to expand the sphere of compliance with its directives. Prestheus posits four bases of legitimation: technical expertise, formal role, rapport and a generalized deference to authority.[29]

Many accept the authority of competent people simply because they are competent. Technical skill and professional attitudes are perhaps the most pervasive criteria for validating authority in the United States. Respect for a superior's expertise as a source of validating his authority is particularly effective where her expertise is in the same area and exceeds that of her subordinates. Specialization strengthens this source of legitimation and professionalization reinforces it.[30]

In a bureaucratic environment, formal position, or role, also serves as a significant basis for the legitimation of authority. It is this sense that most closely approximates Weber's definition of authority. Hierarchy validates authority. Large organizations are often structured to ensure authority by controlling information, centralizing initiative, restricting access to decision-making centers and generally limiting members' behavior. Such psychological inducements as status symbols, rewards and sanctions reinforce the formal allocation of authority. Other conditioning factors include traditions and the mission of the organization. Increasingly, even the great size and specialization of modern organizations encourage greater reliance upon legitimation by hierarchy and formal role.[31]

Authority is also legitimated by interpersonal skill and the work climate executives and supervisors maintain. To the extent that working conditions, pay and career opportunities become standardized, sympathetic human relations tend to become the major distinction between jobs. The warm personality of the boss complements, if not challenges, expert and hierarchical criteria of legitimation. The acceptance of authority has been shown to be positively related to affection for the person who exercises it.[32] Legitimation by rapport serves to blunt the impersonality and routinization of big organizations.[33]

Finally, authority is also legitimated by a generalized deference to it. Individuals are trained from infancy to defer to the authority of parents, teachers, executives and leaders of various kinds. Harry Stack Sullivan posits that one's personality results, in part, from accommodations to authority figures over time, based essentially upon socialization and its compensations.[34] Legitimation by deference is particularly acute in an organizational milieu in which the location of authority and its symbols are clear. In a sense, organizations are systems of roles graded by authority. Titles, income, accessibility, size and decor of office, secretarial buffers and degree of supervision are stimuli that validate authority. Although individuals who occupy the formal roles may change, the "system" of authority relationships persists, again reinforcing deference toward the holder of the position.[35]

Prestheus' four bases of authority have counterparts in the works of others. In Table 2.1, Peabody summarizes the work of five contributors to the study of authority relations in organizations.[36]

Peabody distinguished the bases of formal authority—legitimacy, position and the sanctions inherent in office—from the sources of functional authority—professional competence, experience and human relations skills—because functional authority can support or compete with formal authority. Using this construct, he studied the superordinate-subordinate relationships among 76 of 77 members of three public service organizations: a police department, a welfare office and an elementary school. Peabody found legitimacy and position to have considerable importance as bases of authority in all three organizations, but of more importance to welfare workers. To police officers, authority of person was more frequently important than either authority inherent in position or that derived from superiors. Welfare organization members attached more importance to legitimacy and position than to technical competence and experience as sources of authority. Finally, school employees stressed professional competence as a base of authority much more than either police officers or welfare workers.[37]

Peabody's study highlights two relevant concerns. First, in human service organizations, which the public welfare office more represents than either of the others, it was unexpected to find the extent to which social workers, in contrast to police officers and elementary school teachers, relied on authority of position. Approximately 40% of the 23 public welfare office members mentioned their supervisor as a source of authority, compared to 9% of police and 15% of teachers. As Peabody notes, however, the relatively low degree of importance attributed to authority by competence (22%) for social workers may have been a function

Table 2.1.

Bases of Authority

	Formal Authority		Functional Authority	
	Legitimacy	Position	Competence	Person
Weber	Legal Legal order	Hierarchical	Rational authority Technical knowledge, office	Traditional authority Charismatic authority, experience
Urwick		Formal, conferred by the organization	Technical, implicit in special knowledge or skill	Personal, conferred by seniority or popularity
Simon	Authority of legitimacy, social approval	Authority of sanctions	Authority of confidence (technical competence)	Techniques of persuasion (as distinct from authority)
Bennis		Role incumbency	Knowledge of performance criteria	Knowledge of the human aspect of administration
Presthus	Generalized deference toward authority	Formal role or position	Technical expertise	Rapport with subordinates, ability to mediate individual needs

Source: Reprinted from "Perceptions of Organizational Analysis" by Robert L. Peabody, published in Administrative Science Quarterly, 6 (March, 1962): 467. By permission of Administrative Science Quarterly.

47

of the lack of graduate professional training for all but three members of the staff.[38]

Second, Peabody's study suggested a basic ambivalence, if not an inherent conflict, between the different bases of authority. Approximately 40% of the members in each of the three organizations responded to a question asking whether or not they ever received conflicting instructions from above by giving either a concrete example of authority of competence taking precedent over authority of position or acknowledging the supremacy of authority based on technical skills within certain spheres of their work. Reaction to conflicting instructions from above, typical in the police department and the welfare office and to a lesser extent in the elementary school, was acquiescence to authority of position, particularly among the less experienced members.[39]

In most organizations, there is usually a conflict between formal position and expertise as basis for authority. In organizations with many functions, this conflict is aggravated by a generalist at the top who can rarely be expert in more than one or two functional areas. Those with knowledge in other fields may deny the generalist legitimation of expertise. In complex organizations, problems of authority are often aggravated by the tendency of people to validate authority on the basis of competence in their own fields and to look outside the organization for models of their behavior. This condition affects loyalty to the organization, acceptance of its rules and traditions and the direction of professional energy.[40]

Authority based solely upon formal role is challenged by the groups with conflicting values and assumptions within large organizations. Legitimation by expertise suffers from similar conflict as each group strives to make its own skills and values supreme. Such a professional stalemate results in a power vacuum the generalist fills, again reinforcing the hierarchical basis of authority. More and more frequently, modern organizations, because of their size and number of discrete functional groups, are controlled by generalists. This reflects generalists' (1) monopoly of information and initiative, (2) extended tenure, allowing freedom for tactical maneuver, (3) control of procedural and judicial matters within the organization, (4) absence of any legitimate internal opposition to the "official" policies enunciated by executive staff and (5) mastery over external relations with other managerial elites.[41]

Such control sounds more like power than authority *per se* and contemporary theorists still debate distinctions between the two.[42] As McNeil notes, despite Weber, the sociology of organizations has failed to give priority to the study of organizational power. His concern, however, was with the power relationship organizations had with one another.[43]

Bacharach and Lawler, on the other hand, directly address the concept of power in a way that has a direct bearing on the relationship between authority and information systems and that links these concepts with those of decision making and legitimacy.[44] They note that most theorists view power as a mode of interaction rather than as a structural characteristic independent of and in opposition to the actors engaged in the interaction. As examples, they cite definitions of power by Weber,[45] Blau,[46] Mechanic,[47] Dahl,[48] Kaplan,[49] Bierstedt[50] and Parsons.[51] In their definition, it is not only interactive and relational, but it also connotes dependence. In this, they cite Emerson[52] and Blau,[53] in addition to themselves.[54] Finally, sanctions are inherent to power, particularly the probability of using them and the probability of using them successfully.[55] They posit that analyses of power are embedded in social relationships and relationships can be portrayed in terms of dependence. They argue that the patterns of and degrees of dependence are the basic parameters or delimiters for the context within which actors affect one another. In the dependent relationship, actors confront the issue of when to use sanctions and whether sanctions will be effective with respect to the other party.[56]

Bacharach and Lawler draw upon the works of French and Raven,[57] Raven and Kurglanski,[58] Raven[59] and Etzioni[60] to develop a cogent theoretical framework for the possible bases of power. They distinguish between "bases" of power and "sources" of power. Bases of power refers to the matters in organizational party control which enable the manipulation of the behavior of others. Sources of power, on the other hand, refers to the manner in which those parties come to control the bases of power. As Table 2.2 indicates, Bacharach and Lawler identify four primary bases of power and four sources of power.

The four primary bases of power are: coercion, remuneration, norms and knowledge. The coercive base of power is the control of punishment; remuneration controls rewards; the normative base is the control of symbols; and knowledge is control of information. Any power relationship in an organization can involve any combination of these bases, but one base may characterize any specific relationship.[61]

There are four sources of power: office or structural position, personal characteristics, expertise and opportunity. The first three are roughly equivalent to the bases of authority enumerated by Peabody examined above. The last source of power, opportunity, is provided by the way information flows through the organization. At certain positions, there is access to a significant amount of important information and, generally, there may or may not be formal rules regarding transmission or withholding of this information. This information can be shared with others or withheld. Thus, in addition to the formal chain of communications, informal aspects of formal or informal positions, not identified officially by the organization, can provide an important source of power.[62]

Table 2.2 shows the relationships of the sources, bases and types of power. Most noticeable is the contrast between authority and influence. First, each relies on a different source of power. Authority can only be based on a structural source of power, such as one's office or position in the hierarchy of the organization. Influence, on the other hand, can be grounded in any of the other sources — personality, expertise or opportunity. Second, which of the four bases of power is relevant depends on the power source. Authority can subsume any or all of the four bases of power, while personality can only be supported by normative and knowledge bases and opportunity (information) can only be supported by expertise, coercion and knowledge.[63]

In Table 2.2, Bacharach and Lawler also suggest the formal

Table 2.2.

Relationships of Sources, Bases and Types of Power

Source	Type	Bases
Structure	Authority	Coercion Remunerative Normative Knowledge
Personality	Influence	Normative Knowledge
Expertise	Influence	Normative Knowledge
Opportunity	Influence	Coercion Knowledge

Sources: Samuel B. Bacharach and Edward J. Lawler, Power and Politics in Organizations (San Francisco: Jossey-Bass, Inc., 1980), p. 36.

structure of an organization circumscribes power. Although authority typically has access to a multitude of power bases, on the other hand, there are no clear boundaries of authority formally sanctioned by the organization. The extent of one's authority, hence the degree to which power is circumscribed, can be analyzed in terms of three dimensions: domain, scope and legitimacy.[64]

The domain of authority is the number of units or individuals under the control of a supervisor. The more subgroups or individuals under formal jurisdiction of an individual, the greater the domain of that authority. The scope of one's authority is the range of behaviors or activities controlled for each unit, whether individuals or groups. The wider the range, the greater the scope. The domain and scope of authority typically are well specified and formally defined, while those of influence are generally unclear.[65]

Legitimacy is, perhaps, the most important dimension of authority. Scope and domain are contained in the formal rules underlying authority. Legitimacy, as Weber noted, is a cognitive or perceptual phenomenon, a belief in the appropriateness of the authority structure. Judgments about that appropriateness can be based on moral values, normative ideals or pragmatic or utilitarian criteria. No matter the base, legitimacy implies that subordinates accept both the authority of a superior and the rationale or justification for attaching authority to certain positions and their occupants. The greater the legitimacy attributed to the structure by organizational members, the greater the compliance an organization can command. Legitimacy means subordinates are willing to work within the confines of the existing organizational structure and all members of the organization (regardless of their level in the hierarchy) are willing to follow standard procedures for conducting organizational activities. Since authority implies the right to make the final decision, legitimacy refers specifically to beliefs about rights of decision making.[66]

This discussion of organizational theory and the concept of legitimacy made no attempt to exhaust the literature in this regard.[67] Rather, the focus was on selective and representative works in the field. At this point, a typology can be developed for the distribution of authority, in the formal, structured sense elaborated above, and of the decision load in formal organizations. Bacharach and Lawler provided the direct conceptual link between legitimacy, authority and decision making. What follows is a fuller discussion of decision making and authority within the context of modern organizational theory and the construction of a typology for the legitimate distribution of the decision load.

ORGANIZATIONAL THEORY, DECISION MAKING AND A DECISION-LOAD TYPOLOGY

Organizational Theory and Decision Making

In this section, the material in Chapter 1, the concepts of hierarchical authority and the decision load, will be reviewed. The hierarchy of responsibility, the degree of programmability and the areas of decision make up the decision load. The distribution of decisions within an organization can be examined using these three ideas, and the distribution of the decision load is related to the distribution of authority and needs for information in an organization. To develop our typology, the nature of the relationships of these ideas must be examined in some detail.

The relationships in question occur in an organizational structure. At present, there is no single theory of organizational structure which explains, let alone predicts, the relationship between input and outcome and among levels of responsibility, areas of decision making and distribution of authority.[68] The depiction of formal organizational structure in a table of organization provides a representation of the distribution of authority among the occupants of positions. This distribution can be expressed only in relative terms, comparing one position with another at a given point in time or the same position at different times.[69]

The formal structure also defines areas of accountability. It establishes the zones of performance falling within the competence of a position. The structure provides the range of relationships for a given position. This range, or role set, places individuals in varying degrees of proximity to one another and it sets the boundaries of their expectations. Finally, the formal structure embodies the contract that brings individuals to work. In this sense, it encompasses the motivations which enable people to work together to achieve organizational and personal goals.[70]

In a formal organizational structure, authority can be viewed as prescribed expectations that an individual in a given position should exert control and direction over other individuals within defined areas of competence. In a formal structure, authority becomes active when people begin to communicate intentions and directions for others. It can take many forms and can be altered. Organizational charts or tables represent decisions, generally made by top executives, to distribute authority according to a selected pattern. In a sense, there is an amount of authority, not necessarily fixed, subject to distribution in any organization. There are also different types of authority imbedded in the structure.[71]

Decision making and its processes indicate the distribution of authority, particularly regarding the extent of centralization or decentralization of authority within the formal organizational structure. In a study of 254 city, county and finance departments, Meyer found that, controlling for an organization's size, decision-making authority was more highly centralized as the number of subunits in an organization increased. However, as the number of levels of supervision grew, there was greater decentralization and, concomitantly, a proliferation of rules that specifying criteria for decisions.[72]

Meyer's study links two seemingly disparate traditions in organizational research: the approach of Weber and other classical theorists to the study of organizational structure, which paid little attention to decision-making processes; and Herbert Simon's approach to organizations, concerned primarily with the social psychology of decisions and only tangentially with questions of formal structure. Meyer found support for his link in the vast literature on decentralization and in the continuing debate about the separation of powers in government.[73]

As Meyer points out, as organizations become larger and as the number of hierarchical levels separating the head of the organization from nonsupervisory employees increases, efficiency requires much decision-making authority be removed from top management and given to middle managers. Failure to do this, particularly in organizations with multilevel structures, results in communications overload. In short, increasing vertical division of labor in a bureaucracy or hierarchical division is accompanied by decentralization of authority, which is distributed throughout an organization. In the literature on separation of government powers, there are many descriptions of increasing numbers of subunits reporting directly to the head of government organization, making it more likely that requests for decisions and recommendations will be referred to the top manager, thus centralizing control. In short, the greater the number of subunits or amount of horizontal division of labor in an organization, for instance, functional differentiation between units, the greater the extent to which authority is centralized in the head of the organization.[74]

Meyer also found that functional differentiation tended to centralize decisions in the head of the department; by contrast, hierarchical differentiation between units was associated with delegation of authority to lower levels. The two authority structures, Meyer concluded, have opposite consequences for the distribution of decision-making authority in bureaucratic organizations.[75] In the organizations with centralized authority, the top manager or managers assume a high profile in making decisions about the ordinary operations of the organizations. In centralized authority, not only does top management make policy but it also translates the generalities of that policy into the specifics of command. By contrast, in the pattern of delegated authority, lower-level managers make decisions according to rational principles elaborated by their superiors. In organizations delegating authority, there is a clear separation between those who decided on goals and those who translate them into commands for action, and there are fewer messages transmitted through the hierarchy. Centralized organizations more often rely on competent specialists to receive policies from above and transmit them to subordinates in the form of specific instructions.[76]

Although Meyer painstakingly linked the formal structure of bureaucratic organizations to decision-making processes, in particular to centralization or decentralization of authority, the *de facto* lines of decision making need not coincide with the formal structure of authority. In a study of authority and decision making in a hospital, Coser compared two similarly structured wards, one medical, the other surgical. He showed that the way house doctors made use of the authority attached to their rank differed significantly in the two wards. In the medical ward, consistent delegation of authority down the line allowed the house officers to base their decisions on consensus. On the surgical ward, the chief resident made decisions and issued orders to the surgical officers. Formally, the head nurse on each ward had less authority than the interns, and the surgical head nurse had more decision-making power than the head nurse on the medical unit. Surgical unit house doctors abdicated authority whenever they could rely on the head nurse, who relied less on rules and regulations to support decisions than did the nurses on the medical floor. Thus, despite the formal structure, the manner in which authority was used changed the *de facto* lines of decision making.[77]

Informal decision making is commonplace enough in any formal organization, though it is challenged when those in formal positions of authority "tighten up" the rules and procedures. Thus, the informal system may disrupt or usurp the formal system of authority. In addition, information systems, as part of the formal system, alter the formal process of decision making in an organization. To explore this end, it is helpful to construct a typology to account for the formal hierarchical and functional forms of differentiation in an organization and their relationships to decision making and information needs.

Typology of the Distribution of the Decision Load

Figure 2.1 is a model drawing concepts from various sources discussed above. Classifying managerial control hierarchically (based on Ein-Dor and Segeev's adaptation of Anthony's model) results in division and distribution of decision making, parallel to the levels of formal or hierarchical authority, into operational and managerial modules. Between those modules and the hierarchical levels of authority and decision making is the distribution of the decision load.

This distribution model encompasses the hierarchy or levels of managerial decision making, the functions or levels of program operations and the information needs at each level. Data gathering occurs, for the most part, at the OP or program operations level. Here, information requirements are primarily client characteristics and individual case-by-case service delivery because, at this level, decision making revolves around single cases. The OC or operations control level monitors programmatic output by focusing on the effects of staff activity on clients. The information needed at this level includes the identification and tracking of clients, documentation of service and worker activities, the generation of scheduled reports, and responding to routine inquiries about amount, types and costs of services delivered. Decisions here are made about program modifications and adaptations.[78]

Supervisors and program directors make up the management control center (MCC) opposite the operations control module in Figure 2.1. This level controls both the program's effects on cli-

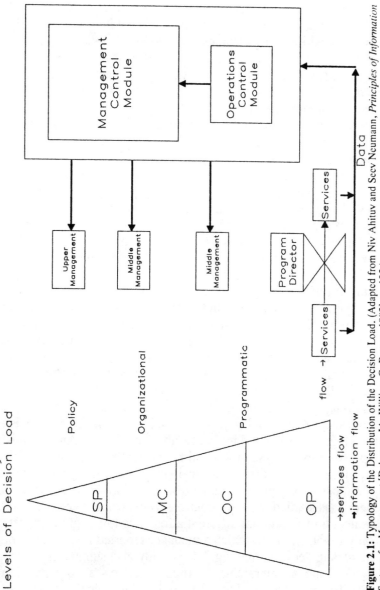

Figure 2.1: Typology of the Distribution of the Decision Load. (Adapted from Niv Ahituv and Seev Neumann, *Principles of Information Systems for Management* [Dubuque, IA: William C. Brown, 1982], p. 135.)

57

ent population and policy decisions affecting service delivery. It includes monitoring reports of service delivery timeliness after clients' initial agency contact, compliance with standards and client dispositions or outcomes. To do this, it relies on aggregate client population data plus supplementary environmental data from external sources for validation of programmatic data and to put it in perspective. Decisions here are made about service needs, organizational constraints on service delivery and improvement of service delivery procedures. Middle managers constitute the group of decision makers who make up the management control centers.

Finally, the policy or top management level focuses on organizational goals, planning objectives, legal actions, responses to legislation, new regulations and other demands on the organization to carry out or modify its functions. At this level, decisions are made about resources used to attain goals and about policies to govern the use of resources. It also focuses on the relationship of the program or agency to the larger environment, which includes funding sources, other programs, demographic changes, the political community and other factors. Decisions here also entail overall policy and priority setting. Top management, which includes Board members as well as the chief executive officer and the top executive staff, make up this group of decision makers. They appear in the management control center opposite the top of the management control module in Figure 2.1.

Although the typology depicted in Figure 2.1 encompasses both hierarchical and functional levels of authority and decision making, it is weighted more heavily to hierarchy. An humanistic approach to administration and management might suggest contrarily, but at least one empirical study found that hierarchy was the most important determinant of the behavior reported for the decisions studied. Span of control, which could be considered an indicator of functional differentiation, was found to be important only to the extent to which a manager reported relying on subordinates in decision making.[79] This study also supported the proposition that an hierarchical structure reflects an organization's distribution of the right to the final decision, whether this is actually choosing among alternatives or formally approving choices already made elsewhere.[80]

The same study also showed upper-level managers have a stronger pattern of reliance on their subordinates and involve them in decision making to a greater degree than managers at lower levels. Lower-level managers had less freedom from superiors and were expected to consult them more often than were upper-level managers and their superiors. In turn, lower-level managers tended not to involve their subordinates in the decision-making process, even though their subordinates were themselves managers in their own right.[81]

This pattern suggests that, at the highest levels of management, there is more participation management and a greater reliance on subordinates by top management. Harmonious relations and committed agreements between top management and subordinates may be a by-product of this participation, as asserted by a humanist approach to management.[82] In modern bureaucracy, however, the combination of technical specialization and the institution of hierarchy dictate otherwise. This has produced an institutional pattern of conflict caused by the growing gap between authority and perception of technical needs.[83] This conflict reflects tensions between professionals and bureaucrats, compounded by the addition of information systems experts into the organization. The foregoing typology hid this conflict. At this point, it is helpful to explore it.

ORGANIZATIONAL CONFLICTS, AUTHORITY AND DECISION MAKING

Conflict in modern organizations can arise from several sources, but Thompson argues that it arises in general from growing inconsistencies between specialist and hierarchical roles. While there are other bases for conflict, it is likely that these could easily be managed under a regime in which specialist solidarity is based upon a mutual recognition of the need for interdependence. This is not likely to occur in most organizations, due to hierarchical structure of authority and reliance on professional staff,[84] a structure which virtually places professionals and bureaucrats at odds with one another.[85]

The term professional, in all its connotations and dimensions refers to a person who, at the least, by virtue of long training is qualified to perform specialized activities autonomously — relatively free of external supervision or regulation. The term bureaucrat, in all its connotations and dimensions refers to a person who, at the least performs, specialized but more routine activities under the supervision of officials organized in a hierarchical fashion. Two very difficult arrangements for organizing work are contained in these two terms, each responding more or less favorably to different sources of authority. As a result, there is at least the possibility of conflict.[86]

Etzioni explores the tension between bureaucrats, whose authority is based on position, and professionals, whose authority is based on knowledge. In his analysis, the most important structural dilemma is the strain imposed on an organization through individual's use of knowledge. In organizations, information is used and relied on more systematically than in other social units. Knowledge is also created and passed from generation to generation. In this instance, Weber overlooked one necessary characteristic of bureaucratic authority. In his view, it is based on technical knowledge or training, while subordinates accept rules and orders as legitimate because they consider being rational being right, and their superiors more rational. In Weber's thought, the higher the rank of an official the better equipped he/she tends to be in either formal education or merit and experience.[87]

Weber's view of bureaucracy, a hierarchy in which the more rational rule the less rational, is undermined by modern organizations for at least two reasons. First, most trained members of most organizations are found not at the highest level but in the middle ranks; not in the regular line or command positions but around them. They are generally referred to as experts, staff, professionals or specialists. Second, the basic principle of administrative authority and the basic principle of professional authority not only are not identical but are quite incompatible.[88]

Administration assumes a power hierarchy, a clear ordering of higher and lower rank in which the higher control and coordinate the latter's activities. Knowledge, however, is largely an individual property and its application is individual in that the professional has ultimate responsibility for any professional decision. Autonomy is necessary for effective professional work. This highly individualized principle is diametrically opposed to the very essence of control and coordination by superiors, i.e., the principle of administrative authority. In short, the ultimate justification for a professional decision is that it is, to the best of his/her knowledge, the correct act. The ultimate justification of an administrative act, however, is that it is in line with the organization's rules and regulations, and has been approved – directly or by implication – by one of a superior rank.[89]

The professional worker in a human service organization serves two masters each at odds with the another: her professional self, with those intellectual and moral criteria, and her employing organization, with its demands and constraints. In his study of professional employees in a bureaucratic structure (public welfare agency), Scott observed that social workers and some social work administrators had different conceptions of the agency and the groups it was designed to serve. The professionals held the client was the prime beneficiary of the services, while the administrators were more concerned with protecting the interests of the public at large, and particularly the taxpayer. This determination of the primary beneficiary of an organization's services, whether the public or the client, is a critical one, and it places bureaucrats and professionals at odds.[90]

The tensions between professionals and bureaucrats are neither new,[91] nor necessarily the same for all bureaucratic structures. Professionals in moderately bureaucratic settings are more likely to perceive themselves as autonomous than those in highly bureaucratic settings.[92] The relationship between the two authority principles – knowledge or administration – differs by type or orientation of an organization. In a full-fledged professional organization such as an university, administrators control secondary activities or administer the means for professionals to carry out the major activity. To the extent there is a staff-line relationship, professionals hold major authority and administrators, secondary staff authority. Administrators advise about economic and organizational implications of various activities planned by professionals. Final decisions are, functionally, made by professionals and their decision-making bodies, such as committees and Boards.[93] This staff-professional line-administrator correlation is reversed in "nonprofessional organizations," such as industrial and military establishments. In these, managers with administrative authority direct the major goal activities. Professionals deal with knowledge as a means, in a subordinate position to managers. In conflicts between the two decision-making apparati, the organizational power structure is slanted in favor of the administrative authority.[94]

Human service organizations are "semiprofessional" in that they are more concerned with the application of knowledge. Here professional activities are coordinated or controlled by those in higher ranks, through organizational regulations and supervision more extensively than in pure professional organizations. The articulation of the two principles of authority is strained,[95] to the extent that the nature of management and service delivery in the human service agency should be examined with particular concern for those aspects made vulnerable by the advent of automated information systems.

SUMMARY

Legitimacy plays an important role in organizational structure and distribution of the decision load. For Weber, the legal-rational type of bureaucratic administration is superior to others. This rests, in part, on its source of legitimacy, which is the legality of enacted rules and the right of those elevated to authority under such rules to issue commands, and in part on the expanded role it gave to technical knowledge. These two factors minimize arbitrary decision making. In a bureaucracy, authority or the capacity to evoke compliance in others, is legitimated by a belief in the correctness of the rules and the loyalty of the bureaucrat is to an impersonal order or superior position, not to the person holding the position.

Critics of Weber broadened the concept of authority. They identified several bases of authority, including legitimacy, position, competence and person, summarized in Table 2.1. These competing bases are often the source of conflict within organizations. Authority based solely on formal role is challenged by conflicting values and assumptions of professional groups in larger organizations. Invariably, this conflict entails disputes about power relationships among competing groups. These disputes are often over scope and domain or parts of the formal rules underlying authority. Some disputes may be over legitimacy or belief in the appropriateness of the authority structure. Legitimacy impels subordinates to be willing to work within the confines of an existing organizational structure and all members of the organization to be willing to follow standard procedures for conducting organizational activities. Authority gives the right to make final decisions and legitimacy describes beliefs about rights of decision making.

At present, there is no theory of organizational structure to explain the relationship among hierarchical levels of responsibility, areas of decision making and the distribution of authority. Figure 2.1 illustrates their relationship, integrating them with information systems. The division and distribution of decision making parallels the levels of formal authority. The decision load is distributed both through the hierarchy of managerial decision making and the functional level of program operations. Some evidence suggests hierarchical position is the most important determinant of decision behavior and upper-level managers tend to involve subordinates in decision-making process to a greater degree than managers at lower levels.

Despite the evidence of greater participation at upper levels, in modern bureaucracies the combination of technical specialization and formal hierarchy encourages conflicts which discourage participation. Organizational conflict can arise from growing inconsistencies between specialist and hierarchical roles. Professionals and bureaucrats respond to different sources of authority. Administration assumes a power hierarchy, a clear ordering of higher and lower rank in which the higher controls and coordinates the latter's activities. The ultimate justification of an administrative act is that it is in line with the organization's rules and regulations approved by a superior. Professionals, however, appeal to their knowledge base for their authority. The ultimate justification for the professional is that it is, to the best of the professional's knowledge, the correct act.

The relationship between the two authority principles, knowledge and administration, differs by type of orientation of an organization. Industry, for example, favors hierarchical authority relations and universities defer more often to the principle of knowledge. Human service organizations contain elements of both in an uneasy partnership, one whose conflicts are exacerbated with the introduction of information systems.

NOTES

1. Claude S. George, *The History of Management Thought* (Englewood Cliffs, NJ: Prentice-Hall, 1972).

2. Robert K. Merton et al. (eds.), *Reader in Bureaucracy* (Glencoe, IL: The Free Press, 1952), p. 17.

3. Carl J. Friedrich, "Some Observations on Weber's Analysis of Bureaucracy," in ibid., p. 27.

4. Nicos P. Mouzelis, *Organization and Bureaucracy: An Analysis of Modern Theories* (Chicago: Aldine, 1967), pp. 16-18. The following descriptive summaries are taken from Max Weber, *Economy and Society*, ed. by Guenther Roth & Claus Wittich, Vols. I and II (Berkeley: University of California Press, 1978), pp. 212-30, 941-1005; Max Weber, *The Theory of Social and Economic Organization*, trans. by A. M. Henderson & Talcott Parsons (New York: The Free Press, 1947), pp. 324-406; and Max Weber, *Basic Concepts in Sociology*, trans. by H. P. Secher (Secaucus, NJ: Citadel Press, 1962), pp. 71-84, 117-18.

5. Weber, *Economy and Society*, Vol. I, p. 215.

6. Weber, *Basic Concepts in Sociology*, p. 82.

7. Weber, *Economy and Society*, Vol. I, p. 82.

8. Weber, *The Theory of Social and Economic Organization*, p. 324.

9. Ibid., pp. 329-30.

10. Ibid., pp. 330-32.

11. Ibid., pp. 333-34.

12. Ibid., p. 337.

13. Ibid., pp. 337-39.

14. Weber, *Economy and Society*, Vol. II, p. 975.

15. Stanley Udy, " 'Bureaucratic' Elements in Organizations: Some Research Findings," "Research Reports and Notes," *American Sociological Review*, 23 (August, 1958): 415-418.

16. Herbert Simon, *Administrative Behavior* (2nd ed.; New York: Macmillan, 1962), pp. 26-28.

17. Mouzelis, *Organization and Bureaucracy*, p. 40.

18. Ibid., p. 42.

19. Ibid., p. 43; Talcott Parsons, "Suggestions for a Sociological Approach to the Theory of Organizations," *Administrative Science Quarterly*, 1 (June and September, 1956): 63-75 and 224-39. See also, Talcott Parsons, *Structure and Processes in Modern Societies* (Glencoe, IL: The Free Press, 1960), pp. 16-58; and Talcott Parsons, "Social Systems," in *The Sociology of Organizations*, ed. by Oscar Grusky & George A. Miller (2nd ed.; New York: The Free Press, 1981), pp. 98-109.

20. Herbert Simon, *Administrative Behavior* (2nd ed.; New York: Macmillan, 1957), p. xxxiv-xxxv.

21. Peter Blau, "Critical Remarks on Weber's Theory of Authority," *American Political Science Review*, 57 (June, 1963): 305-16.

22. Ibid., p. 312.

23. Robert V. Presthus, "Authority in Organizations," *Public Administration Review*, 20 (Spring, 1960): 87.

24. R. Kippott, N. Polansky & S. Rosen, "The Dynamics of Power," *Human Relations*, 5 (February, 1952): 44-50.

25. Chester I. Barnard, *The Functions of the Executive* (Cambridge, MA: Harvard University Press, 1938), p. 163.

26. Presthus, "Authority in Organizations," p. 87. See also Morris Janowitz, "Changing Patterns of Organizational Authority: The Military Establishment," *Administrative Science Quarterly*, 3 (March, 1959): 473-93; and N. Kaplan, "The Role of the Research Administrator," *Administrative Science Quarterly*, 4 (June, 1959): 20-42.

27. J. Block & J. Block, "An Interpersonal Experiment on Relations to Authority," *Human Relations*, 5 (February, 1952): 91-98.

28. Herbert A. Simon, "Authority," in *Research in Industrial Human Relations*, ed. by C. Arensberg (New York: Harper and Brothers, 1957), p. 106.

29. Prestheus, "Authority in Organizations," pp. 88-91.

30. Robert V. Prestheus, "The Social Bases of Organization," *Social Forces*, 38 (December, 1959): 103-09.

31. Prestheus, "Authority in Organizations," p. 88.

32. R. P. French and R. Snyder, "Leadership and Interpersonal Power," in

Studies in Social Power, ed. by D. Cartwright (Ann Arbor: University of Michigan Institute for Social Research, 1959), pp. 118-49.

33. Prestheus, "Authority in Organizations," p. 89.

34. Henry Stack Sullivan, "Tensions, Interpersonal and International," in *Tensions That Cause Wars,* ed. by H. Cantril (Urbana: University of Illinois, 1950), p. 95.

35. Prestheus, "Authority in Organizations," 90-91.

36. Robert L. Peabody, "Perceptions of Organizational Authority: A Comparative Analysis," *Administrative Science Quarterly,* 6 (March, 1962): 467. The sources that Peabody uses for each of the contributors are Weber, *The Theory of Social and Economic Organization,* pp. 328, 339; L. Urwick, *The Elements of Administration* (New York: Harper and Brothers, 1944), p. 42; Simon, "Authority," pp. 104-06 and H. A. Simon, D. W. Smithburg & V. A. Thompson, *Public Administration* (New York: 1950), pp. 189-201; Warren G. Bennis, "Leadership Theory and Administrative Behavior: The Problems of Authority," *Administrative Science Quarterly,* 4 (September, 1959): 288-89; and Prestheus, "Authority in Organizations," 88-91.

37. Peabody, op. cit., 477.

38. Ibid., 480.

39. Ibid., 481-482.

40. Prestheus, "Authority in Organizations," 89.

41. Ibid.; Robert Michels, *Political Parties: A Study of Oligarchical Tendencies in Modern Democracy* (New York: The Free Press, 1949).

42. See Paul M. Harrison, "Weber's Categories of Authority and Voluntary Associations," *American Sociological Review,* 25 (April, 1960): 232-37; and "On Power and Authority: An Exchange on Concepts," Communications, *American Sociological Review,* 25 (October, 1960): 731-32.

43. Kenneth McNeil, "Understanding Organizational Power: Building on the Weberian Legacy," *Administrative Science Quarterly,* 23 (March, 1978): 65-90.

44. Samuel B. Bacharach & Edward J. Lawler, *Power and Politics in Organizations: The Social Psychology of Conflict, Coalitions, and Bargaining* (San Francisco: Jossey-Bass, 1980).

45. Weber, *The Theory of Social and Economic Organizations,* p. 152.

46. Peter M. Blau, *Exchange and Power in Social Life* (New York: Wiley, 1964).

47. David Mechanic, "Sources of Power of Lower Participants in Complex Organizations," *Administrative Science Quarterly,* 7 (December, 1962): 351.

48. Robert A. Dahl, "The Concept of Power," *Behavioral Science,* 2 (July, 1957): 201-18.

49. A. Kaplan, "Power in Perspective," in *Power and Conflict in Organization,* ed. by R. L. Kahn & E. Boulding (London: Tavistock, 1964), p. 11-32.

50. R. Bierstedt, "An Analysis of Power," *American Sociological Review*, 15 (December, 1950): 730-38.

51. Talcott Parsons, "Suggestions for a Sociological Approach to the Theory of Organizations."

52. R. M. Emerson, "Power Dependence Relations," *American Sociological Review*, 27 (February, 1962): 31-40; "Exchange Theory, Part II: Exchange Relations, Exchange Networks, and Groups as Exchange Systems," in *Sociological Theories in Progress*, ed. by J. Berger, M. Zelditch & B. Anderson (Vol. 2; Boston: Houghton Mifflin, 1972).

53. Blau, *Exchange and Power in Social Life*.

54. Samuel B. Bacharach & Edward J. Lawler, "The Perception of Power," *Social Forces*, 55 (September, 1976): 123-34; "Power Tactics in Bargaining" (Ithaca, NY: New York State School of Industrial and Labor Relations, Cornell University, 1980).

55. See Dahl, "The Concept of Power;" W. A. Gamson, "Power and Probability," in *Perspective on Social Power*, ed. by J. D. Tedeschi (Chicago: Aldine, 1974); and Denis H. Wrong, "Some Problems in Defining Social Power," *American Journal of Sociology*, 76 (May, 1968): 673-81.

56. Bacharach & Lawler, *Power and Politics in Organizations*, pp. 15-26.

57. J. R. French & B. H. Raven, "The Bases of Social Power," *Studies in Social Power*, ed. by D. Cartwright (Ann Arbor: University of Michigan Press, 1959).

58. B. H. Raven & A. W. Kruglanski, "Conflict and Power," in *The Structure of Conflict*, ed. by P. Swingle (New York: Academic Press, 1970).

59. B. H. Raven, "A Comparative Analysis of Power and Power Preference," in *Perspectives on Social Power*, ed. by J. T. Tedeschi.

60. Amatai Etzioni, *A Comparative Analysis of Complex Organizations* (New York: The Free Press, 1961).

61. Bacharach & Lawler, *Power and Politics in Organizations*, p. 34.

62. Ibid., pp. 34-36; Mechanic, "Sources of Power in Lower Participants in Complex Organizations."

63. Bacharach & Lawler, op. cit., pp. 36-38.

64. Ibid., p. 38.

65. Ibid.

66. Ibid., p. 39.

67. For more systematic and historical treatment of various schools of thought like the classical approach vis-à-vis the human relations approach to the study of bureaucracy and organizations, see Mouzelis, *Organization and Bureaucracy*. See also Jerald Hage, *Theories of Organizations: Form, Process, and Transformation* (New York: Wiley, 1980); Mason Haire, ed., *Modern Organization Theory: A Symposium of the Foundation for Research on Human Behavior* (New York: Wiley, 1959); and Charles Perrow, *Complex Organizations: A Critical Essay* (2nd ed.; New York: Random House, 1979).

68. Input refers to such resources as personnel, finances, facilities, equipment and the like. Outcome refers to the *results* of organizational efforts and represent the achievement of goals.

69. Gene W. Dalton et al., *The Distribution of Authority in Formal Organizations* (Boston: Graduate School of Business Administration, Division of Research, Harvard University, 1968), p. 2.

70. Ibid., pp. 2-3.

71. Ibid., pp. 35-39.

72. Marshall W. Meyer, "The Two Authority Structures of Bureaucratic Organization," *Administrative Science Quarterly*, 13 (September, 1968): 211-28.

73. Ibid., p. 213.

74. Ibid., pp. 214-25.

75. Ibid., p. 222.

76. Ibid., pp. 225-27.

77. Rose Laub Coser, "Authority and Decision-Making in a Hospital: A Comparative Analysis," *American Sociological Review*, 23 (February, 1958): 56-63. In so doing, Coser corroborated Merton's formulation in "Social Structure and Anomie," i.e., that "some social structures exert a definite pressure upon certain persons in the society to engage in nonconformist rather than conformist conduct." See Robert K. Merton, *Social Theory and Social Structure* (1968 enlarged ed.; New York: The Free Press, 1967), pp. 185-214.

78. Gruber et al., "Information Management," *Human Services at Risk: Administrative Strategies for Survival*, ed. by Felice Perlmutter (Lexington, MA: Lexington Books, 1984), p. 131; Jolie Bain Pillsbury & Kathy Newton Nance, "An Evaluation Framework for Public Welfare Agencies," *Public Welfare*, 34 (Winter, 1976): 48-50.

79. L. Vaughn Blankenship & Raymond E. Miles, "Organizational Structure and Managerial Decision Behavior," *Administrative Science Quarterly*, 13 (June, 1968): 106.

80. Victor A. Thompson, "Hierarchy, Specialization, and Organizational Conflict," *Administrative Science Quarterly*, 5 (March, 1961): 485-521.

81. Blankenship & Miles, "Organizational Structure and Managerial Decision Behavior," p. 110.

82. Harold J. Leavitt, "Applied Organization Change in Industry: Structural, Technical, and Human Approaches," in *New Perspectives in Organization Research*, ed. W. W. Cooper et al. (New York: Wiley, 1964), pp. 69-70.

83. Thompson, "Hierarchy, Specialization, and Organizational Conflict," p. 485.

84. Victor A. Thompson, *Modern Organization* (New York: Alfred A. Knopf, 1961), p. 109.

85. Paul D. Montagna, "Professionalization and Bureaucratization in

Large Professional Organizations," *American Journal of Sociology*, 74 (September, 1968): 138-45.

86. W. Richard Scott, "Professional Employees in a Bureaucratic Structure: Social Work," in *The Semi-Professions and Their Organization: Teachers, Nurses, Social Workers*, ed. by Amitai Etzioni (New York: The Free Press, 1969), pp. 82-83.

87. Amatai Etzioni, *Modern Organizations* (Englewood Cliffs, NJ: Prentice-Hall, 1964), pp. 75-76; Weber, *The Theory of Social and Economic Organization*, p. 339.

88. Etzioni, op. cit., p. 76.

89. Ibid., pp. 76-77.

90. Scott, "Professional Employees in a Bureaucratic Structure," p. 131.

91. Barry D. Karl, "Public Administration and American History: A Century of Professionalism," *Public Administration Review* (September/October, 1976): 489-503.

92. Gloria V. Engel, "Professional Autonomy and Bureaucratic Organization," *Administrative Science Quarterly*, 15 (March, 1970): 12-21.

93. Etzioni, *Modern Organizations*, pp. 81-82.

94. Ibid., pp. 79-81.

95. Ibid., pp. 87-89.

Chapter 3

Human Service Agencies: Their Nature, Structure and Management

Human service organization is a loosely used term for those not-for-profit organizations in the public and private sectors which fall under the rubrics of health, education and welfare.[1] They run the gamut of organization types from United Way to family service agencies, to Planned Parenthood, to public welfare and other large-scale public organizations.[2] The range and diversity of such organizations make it quite difficult to speak of them as a uniform phenomenon. They vary in size, goals, nature of authority, patterns of communication and relationship to the marketplace.[3] Nonetheless, there are some common characteristics which separate human service organizations from other types.[4]

First, human service organizations work for people by processing and/or changing them individually or collectively. The clients of these organizations simultaneously constitute their input, raw materials and product. Decisions and actions undertaken by these organizations involve moral evaluation and judgment of people and, thereby, have consequences on their normative values and social standing. Even though most human service organizations adopt ideological systems to justify their activities, they continuously face the risk these ideologies might be contested by various social groups.

Second, human service organizations are characterized by muddled missions. Because they intervene in the lives of people, they are confronted with multiple expectations and conflicting demands in a pluralistic society. For example, public welfare agencies simultaneously provide for the needs of the poor, while they face the demand to reduce welfare rolls and encourage the poor to enter the labor market. Similarly, juvenile courts pursue goals of "law and order" and "social rehabilitation." To accommodate conflicting demands, human service organizations often develop ambiguous, if not contradictory, goals.

Third, human service organizations are highly dependent on resources controlled by other organizations, often through extensive legislative and administrative regulations. This dependency fosters development of service modalities reflecting the constraints and contingencies imposed by external units, rather than actual needs of the population.

And, fourth, despite the increase in new service methods, human service organizations lack determinate and effective technologies. Most human service methods are based on limited and fragmentary knowledge bases. They fail to meet the accepted attributes of a technology[5] and few can be shown to be effective.[6] Consequently, human service organizations develop ideological systems in lieu of technologies to guide and justify the behavior of staff. Indeterminate methods allow a great deal of staff discretion, compounding problems inherent in quality control. Development of explicit criteria for performance assessment and measures of accountability become highly problematic.[7]

These four aspects of human service organizations are more useful as delimiters than the more traditional breakdown into profit and nonprofit.[8] By and large, human service organizations are nonprofit, forming a large subset of all nonprofit organizations. These four delimiting aspects of human service organizations have a direct bearing on the functions of management and the uses of information within them.

THE NATURE OF HUMAN SERVICE TECHNOLOGIES AND ORGANIZATIONS

Hasenfeld identifies five attributes or characteristics of human service technologies illustrating the ideological principles guiding service delivery and the rational criteria guiding information management.[9]

First, human service methods can be viewed as moral systems. As clients move through the organizational process, aspects of their biographies acquire new social meanings, confirming or altering their moral status. When a social worker, for example, decides a client needs to acquire better child rearing skills, that decision invariably generates a social meaning affecting not only the valuation of (and response to) the client by that worker and others, but also the client's own identity. Second, human services technology can be viewed as indeterminate systems. The inability to control for extraneous factors and invisible or unknown processes often makes it exceedingly difficult to attribute the observed consequences to the effects of a given process. The lack of a clear relationship between a given set of intervention procedures and outcomes allows proliferation of many variations and practices under the guise of the same method, an ambiguity which raises issues concerning its exclusivity.

Third, those attributes result in difficulties in selecting appropriate methods, in part because they might not exist, in part because competing ones may have various degrees of support in scientific knowledge, and because they encourage the elevation of certain moral values over and above empirical validity. For example, behavioral modification techniques may be scientifically valid, but clash with values one wishes to promote. Thus, practitioners adopt practice ideologies. Rapoport defines practice ideologies as "formal systems of ideas that are held with great tenacity and emotional investment, that have self-confirming features, and that are resistant to change from objective rational reappraisal. . . . Ideology welds observable aspects of the environment into a kind of unit by filling in gaps in knowledge with various projections that ultimately supply a coherent belief system on which action can be based and justified."[10] Practice ideologies perform a dual function for an organization. They reduce uncertainty by offering consistent courses of action and they provide rationale and justification for staff actions with clients.[11]

Thus, ideologies as a basis for intervention techniques have important consequences for human service organizations. First, because ideologies are abstract belief systems beset by internal inconsistencies and ambiguities, many practice principles may be justified under the same ideology. This lack of one-to-one correspondence between ideology and action allows practitioners considerable discretion in client interaction. Second, ideologies are self-confirming, allowing practitioners to reify models of human behavior, which leads to self-fulfilling prophecies. When psychotherapists, for example, assume lower-class clients are unable to benefit from psychotherapy, they are more likely to display discomfort during treatment. This results in the premature termination of these clients from psychotherapy and confirms the psychotherapists' original assumptions.[12] Finally, ideologies tend to be barriers to innovation, filtering out incompatible knowledge as inadmissible and unacceptable to the organization.[13]

A fourth characteristic of human service methods is reliance on face-to-face interactions. This reliance causes considerable discretion to be invested in line staff. Much information about clients and their needs is transmitted to the organization by line staff, and much information about organizational policies and services available to clients is also controlled by them. Lipsky called line staff "street level bureaucrats," whose work is characterized by the following conditions: (1) they are in constant interaction with clients; (2) they have comparative independence and discretion, and their own personal attitudes and behavior may significantly affect the client's treatment; and (3) they can have a marked impact on their clients.[14]

Reliance on personal contact, in many ways, contradicts the bureaucratic principles governing the structure and processes of human service organizations. Those principles promote universalism, affective neutrality, specificity and restraint. Face-to-face interaction, however, encourages particularism, affective involvement, diffuseness of relations and discretion. The human service practitioners, hence, experience conflicting role expectations from the organization and from clients.[15]

Finally, human service methods can be viewed as client control systems. All human service organizations must minimize clients' ability to negate efforts to transform their behaviors and feelings. Patients may refuse to comply with a physician's orders; students may ignore their teachers; and clients may resist discussing their interpersonal problems. The need for client compliance and cooperation is particularly heightened when the method aims at some major changes in the client's behavior and when it requires active client participation and involvement. Face-to-face interaction increases the organization's dependency on the client's compliance. Consequently, control of the client and elicited conformity are critical issues in human service organizations, consuming much effort from practitioners. [16]

Those five attributes are common to three major types or functions of human service systems: people-processing, people-sustaining and people-changing. People-processing methods are exemplified in the processes of juvenile courts, credit-rating bureaus or testing and diagnosing units. They have one central purpose, to confer on people a particular social label, social position, or status which will, in turn, produce a predetermined response from significant social groups or organizations. People-sustaining systems are exemplified in the processes of welfare departments, nursing homes or hospital chronic wards. Their central aim is to prevent, arrest or delay the deterioration of a person's well-being or social status. And, people-changing systems are exemplified in the processes of educational programs, psychotherapy, family counseling or physical rehabilitation. They aim directly at altering clients' biophysical, psychological or social attributes in order to improve their well-being and social functioning. [17] Table 3.1 summarizes the major distinctions between people-processing, people-sustaining and people-changing systems.

Of particular importance here is the distinction between managerial concerns. Disposition or the linking of the client to other units is a primary managerial concern to an organization engaged in people-processing. Ensuring a smooth flow of people in and out of the processing unit and avoiding a backlog is a major factor, shaping the activities of staff. Acceptable allocation rules — the guidelines and procedures prescribing the variety, amount and frequency of support and care clients will obtain from the

Table 3.1.

A Typology of the Functions of Human Services Technologies

	People Processing	People Sustaining	People Changing
Type of Product Core Activities	Altered status Classification-disposition	Attribute stabilization Custodial care; sustentation	Attribute change Planned change
Organizational Locus	Boundaries	Intrapartial insulation	Intramaximal insulation
Managerial Concern	Disposition of product	Acceptable allocation of rules	Demonstrated effectiveness
Staff-Client Relations Client Control	Minimal Threats and promises;	Modest Threats and promises promises reinforcement control	Extensive Persuasion; reinforcement control
Staff Compliance	Bureaucratic	Bureaucratic	Commitment

Source: Yeheskel Hasenfeld, Human Service Organizations, copyright 1983, Adapted by permission of Prentice-Hall, Inc., Englewood Cliffs, New Jersey.

organization—is a primary managerial concern to an organization engaged in people-sustaining. Enforcement of standard operating procedures and uniformly applied criteria for providing care are the major mechanics used to minimize the inherent potential for neglect and abuse of clients. This minimizes staff discretion in services they control. Finally, demonstrated effectiveness is a major administrative concern in organizations engaged in people-changing technologies. Entrusting core activities to professionals enables an organization to protect its methods from external inspection and proclaim effectiveness on the basis of professional judgment.[18]

Rationality pervades these three types of methods and is supported by current theory and research on organizational structure which demonstrate how arrangement of activities, distribution of authority and control of work flow are guided by a norm of rationality.[19] Whether such an approach is applicable to human service organizations, however, is problematic for several reasons. First, human service organizations face turbulent environments, characterized by multiple, often conflicting goals which severely constrain their ability to design rational internal structures.

Second, human service methods incorporate many tasks and activities whose definitions and specifications vary widely among organizations and among practitioners. The internal structure of an agency readily cannot be guided by a systematic blueprint when it is subject to these ideological vagaries. Third, human service technologies have difficulty in monitoring and evaluating staff performance and output. These difficulties emanate, in part, from the vagueness of the technologies, the complexity of human attributes, the low visibility of staff activities and the indeterminacy of output goals. Yet effective control of an organization is contingent on the existence of an explicit and acceptable evaluation scheme.

Finally, staff-client encounters, the predominant activity in human service organizations, are not readily subject to organizational control since they are vulnerable to the vicissitudes of both clients and line staff. Consequently, efforts to structure and control these encounters to accord with organizational policies are likely to be wrought with difficulties.[20] These nonrational aspects of human service organizations affect both the distribution of power and the exercise of authority in them. An appreciation of this relationship is necessary to an understanding of how the development and implementation of a management information system can alter the structures and processes of authority in human service organizations.

POWER AND AUTHORITY
IN THE HUMAN SERVICE ORGANIZATION

In one sense, the power of an organization's members is a function of the amount of resources they control. The power of a unit (whether an individual or a group) varies directly with the organization's need for the resources controlled by that unit and inversely with the availability of that resource elsewhere. Resources may be money, legitimation, clients, expertise, manpower or information. An organization's relative need for each resource and its availability will vary over time, and power will shift among units which control access to it.[21]

Hinings and others have proposed the following steps of attaining power in an organization: (1) the unit, either individuals or staff groups, enters an area of high uncertainty for the organization, which might be procurement of resources or attainment of a specific technical proficiency; (2) the unit effectively copes with that uncertainty; (3) no other unit can provide a substitute for the skills acquired by that unit; and (4) the unit's activities become central to the performance of other units.[22]

Individuals and groups in the organization can use initial power to generate more by seizing control of activities meeting the above conditions. Lorber and Satow note that those psychiatrists who dominated a community mental health center by their reputation and prestige defined the preferred treatment method to be psychoanalytically oriented therapy, the one in which they had the most expertise.[23] Consequently, that form of therapy was accorded the highest prestige in the agency, and clients amenable to it perceived as most desirable. The least preferred therapy — provision of concrete services — was delegated to paraprofessionals.[24]

Power may also be acquired by possessing special skills and expertise essential to the management or controlling a core system, one not readily replaced. In a comparative analysis of juvenile correctional institutions, Zald found cottage parents in custodial institutions were perceived to have more power than social workers, while in individual-treatment centers, the opposite was true. In milieu-treatment institutions, which required a "team" approach, both groups were perceived as having equal power.[25]

Power is also attained or acknowledged by possessing formal authority. Recognizing differing importance of various tasks and their requisite skills and expertise, an organization differentially allocates formal authority to the positions. In particular, increased authority is granted to those with responsibility over tasks which direct and coordinate the activities of others. As noted in Chapter 1, power inherent in formal authority is a function of the weight of the legal sanctions attached to it and its endorsement by subordinates. That is, the amount of authority a position holder in an organization can exercise depends on (1) the importance and severity of the legal sanctions at his or her disposal and (2) the acceptance by subordinates of the legitimacy, appropriateness and fairness of the directives he/she issues. For example, social workers may attempt to circumvent the authority of supervisors if their directives are perceived to be unfair or inappropriate.[26]

The distribution of authority in an organization is inherently hierarchical. Many regard this as a universal characteristic of organizations; some empirical studies of diverse organizations in different countries support such a proposition.[27] Authority's importance in granting power to its holders must be stressed. Even in professional organizations, individuals with hierarchical authority are more likely to participate in decision making.[28] This is particularly evident in times of crisis, when formal authority is magnified as the source of decisions moves up in the hierarchy.[29]

In general, the congruence between formal authority and the

exercise of power will be greater in tightly coupled than in loosely coupled organizations. The former, characterized by a stable environment and a determinate technology, can establish an authority structure not challenged by change, ambiguity and uncertainty. By contrast, in loosely coupled organizations, the formal authority structure is constantly undermined by environmental uncertainty, goal ambiguity and technological indeterminacy. In loosely coupled organizations, incongruity exists between the formal authority system and the actual distribution of power. The same factors which shape the internal structure and the distribution of power in human service organizations generate considerable divergence between possession of formal authority and the actual exercise of power. Hospital attendants and nurses, for example, exercise more power over their patients than indicated by their formal authority.[30] And, welfare workers exercise more discretion than officially permitted.[31]

Professional status also provides another way to secure power and enhance authority. It provides links to external sources of legitimation, prestige and reputation, as well as control over a body of knowledge and skills not readily replaced. The power and authority of a profession emanate from two sources. First, a profession undertakes a domain of activities incorporating a high degree of uncertainty, both because of the nature of the activities and the complexity and incompleteness of the body of knowledge.[32] Second, the state grants professions rights to the services and knowledge to which they lay claim.[33] A profession obtains these rights by accommodating state control of deviants, maintenance of dominant values and ideologies and general support of the political system. The state, in turn, delegates some of its power to the profession, permitting it to regulate itself while providing protection from encroachment by other occupational groups.[34]

By and large, professional power and authority are manifested through ability of the profession to determine and control the conditions of their work and to attain autonomy from organizational evaluation and administrative authority. Accordingly, human service occupations vary in their employment of professionals. These range from physicians, who enjoy, perhaps, the highest degree of professional status, to social workers, teachers and nurses, to hospital attendants, eligibility workers and prison guards. This employment, as noted in Chapter 2, poses a potential conflict between professional autonomy and bureaucratic authority.[35] On the whole, however, organizations develop an internal structure which facilitates the work of the professional, while preserving overall administrative coordination.[36]

In general, professionals are subject to hierarchical authority in areas which fall outside their sphere, such as scheduling and setting fees, while their authority becomes advisory on professional matters. Organizations formalize and standardize regulative rules, those pertaining to personal management, requisition of resources and equipment, and reporting, but not to operative rules, or those pertaining to actual work done.[37] There are some professional groups, however, such as social workers, whose claims for exclusive control over a sphere of activities and knowledge are often challenged by administrative authority, and sometimes by more prestigious professionals.

In contrast to the advisory model of bureaucracy, professional and administrative authority tend to blur in social work agencies. Supervisors are often colleagues who have become administrators and blend both administrative and professional criteria in their evaluation and exercise of authority. As Ruzik notes, ". . . social work administrators and supervisors judge and evaluate their 'colleagues' on the basis of agency, rather than purely professional goals."[38] The conflicting demands stemming from professional and administrative concerns further compound management, decision making and the use of information in human service agencies.

MANAGEMENT AND DECISION MAKING IN HUMAN SERVICE ORGANIZATIONS

Myron Weiner argues that human services management differs significantly from that in other types of organizations in three aspects: (1) all human service organizations serve multifaceted, complex people who are increasingly being viewed in comprehensive holistic terms; (2) the natural setting for human service organizations is interorganizational in nature; and (3) the environment within which human services provide opportunities and services is dynamic and changing at such a pace that recording it is nearly impossible.[39]

These factors cause human service organizations to be more like "organized anarchies" than rational structures. That is, these organizations can be characterized by problematic preferences, unclear methods, and fluid participation. Human service organizations have a variety of inconsistent and ill-defined preferences, shown by the multiplicity of goals and objectives and the global nature of mission statements. They rely heavily on unclear methods, trial and error procedures, residues of learning from accidents of past experience and pragmatic inventions. And, finally, in human service organizations, participants vary in the amount of time and effort they devote to different aspects of the organization. By and large, the boundaries of the organization are uncertain and in flux; the audiences and decision makers for any particular kind of choice change capriciously.[40] How then are decisions made and information used in human service organizations?

Like many loaded questions, an answer to this depends on one's perspective. In this case, it is through organizational behavior theory. Organizations can be examined, as Burton Gummer does, through three different perspectives or models of behavior: the rational, the natural system and power politics.[41] As Table 3.2 indicates, there are major variables and dynamics in each.

The extensive discussion of organizational theories and decision making in previous chapters, leads to a discussion of organizational decision making and the way human service administrators and practitioners typically obtain and use information in their daily work. Such an approach combines aspects of each work model.

Rather than a single, well-specified objective, most human

Table 3.2.

Major Variables and Dynamics in the Rational,

Natural-System, and Power-Politics Models of Organizations

	Rational	Natural-System	Power-Politics
Variables	Production goals Technologies	Subsystem goals Informal structure	Resource characteristics Control structure
Dynamics	Maximization of rationality Reduction of uncertainty	Management of internal conflict Maintenance of the character of the system	Adaptation to changes in resource availability

Source: Burton Gummer, "Organization Theory for Social
Administration," in Leadership in Social Administration,
ed. by Felice Davidson Perlmutter and Simon Slavin
(Philadelphia: Temple University Press, 1980), p. 23.

service organizations have several objectives, imperfectly stated as broad, vague, general goals. Groups, in various coalitions, within the organization have a dominant influence over resources. A definition of the organizational tasks accompanies this control; this, in turn, rationalizes the allocation of assignments to divisions or groups as well as the rewards received. To attain an organization's goals, a system that takes in information about its activities and its environment is essential. It must be one to filter, process and communicate such information and render possible decisions to guide the behavior of the participants. This system must follow more or less regular patterns or sequences. Yet organizational processes are shaped by such factors as the distribution of influence, authority and power among the participants; negotiated objectives; commonly accepted operating procedures for work; and general guidelines for responding to novel situations.[42]

Some can argue, as Cohen et al.[43] and Holland[44] do, whether a search for information postdates or precedes the search for a solution to a specific problem. Regardless, the screen through which organizational participants define problems and assess solutions is biased by training, values, interests and goals. Basically, proposed solutions and defined problems are filtered for proximity to existing goals and minimizing disturbance to existing assumptions and distributions of influence, authority and power. Such screens serve both to ward off new explanations and to maintain the existing structure of authority and styles of behavior.[45]

Human service organizations seldom examine their decision-making processes and the information needed, let alone the kinds of information needed to support the various types of decisions managers and practitioners make. Furthermore, the role and importance of information, short of what is needed to secure funds from government or United Way, is still open-ended. Other organizational priorities frequently eclipse those of gathering and using information systematically and rationally, as can "political factors."[46]

In most human service organizations, information collection

and use are basically informal rather than systematic, goal-directed processes, often intended primarily for meeting funding requirements. Decision making is far from routine or rational in the usual sense of that term. The kinds of information most often used in planning and management decisions are usually not collected in any systematic, goal-directed manner over time. Most decision making is heavily influenced, if not determined, by filters composed of political and value-oriented factors. They are oriented toward several objectives simultaneously, only some of which are overt, explicit and consistent with other organizational goals. Invariably, automated information systems involve the superimposition of a rational process upon these basically quasi-rational procedures. Breakdowns occur when the quantitative and routinized aspects of the technical systems do not fit with the qualitative needs of decision makers and practitioners.[47]

It should be noted, however, that human service managers and practitioners do more than "muddle through," despite the uncertainty of their environments, the complexity of their clients, the relevant political factors, the fuzziness of objectives and the like. Lindblom's comparison of two approaches to administrators' formulation of policy is instructive.[48] Table 3.3 illustrates the characteristics of both the rational-comprehensive method and successive limited comparisons method.

Many characteristics of the successive limited comparisons model closely approximate the dynamics of decision making in human service organizations. Particularly, value goals and analysis of needed action are intertwined, and there is reliance on successive comparisons with past experiences instead of reliance on theory. This comparison, however, is not meant to suggest that decisions made by managers and practitioners either defy rationality or lack rigor. Donald Schon is indebted to Chris Argyris[49] for his analysis of the distinctive structure of the phenomenon he calls "reflection-in-action," common to such professionals as psychotherapists, engineers and managers.[50] Human service organizations abound with reflective practitioners, managers and providers of direct service.[51]

Technical rationality depends on agreement about ends. When

Table 3.3.

Rational-Comprehensive and Successive Limited

Comparisons Models of Policy Formation

Rational-Comprehensive Model

1. Clarification of values or objectives distinct from and usually prerequisite to empirical analysis of alternative policies.

2. Policy formulation is therefore approached through means-end analysis: First the ends are isolated, then the means to achieve them are sought.

3. The test of a "good" policy is that it can be shown to be the most appropriate means to desired ends.

4. Analysis is comprehensive; every important relevant factor is taken into account.

5. Theory is often heavily relied upon.

Successive Limited Comparisons Model

1. Selection of value goals and empirical analysis of the needed action are not distinct from one another but are closely intertwined.

2. Since means and ends are not distinct, means-end analysis is often inappropriate or limited.

3. The test of a "good" policy is typically that various analysts find themselves directly agreeing on a policy (without their agreeing that it is the most appropriate means to an agreed objective).

4. Analysis is drastically limted:

    a. Important possible outcomes are neglected.

    b. Important alternative potential policies are neglected.

    c. Important affected values are neglected.

5. A succession of comparisons greatly reduces or eliminates reliance on theory.

Source: Adapted from Charles E. Lindblom, "The Science of Muddling Through,'" Public Administration Review, 19 (Spring, 1959): 81.

ends are fixed and clear, then the decision to act becomes an instrumental problem. But, when ends are confused and conflicting, there is as yet no "problem" to solve. Hence, there is credibility in the "garbage can" model of decision making. It posits, among other things, that agreed upon solutions, in short, search and find problems they can solve.[52] As noted previously, one aspect of human service organizations is their indeterminate methods. When there are conflicting paradigms of professional practice, as in social work and administration, there is no clearly established context for the use of technique. There is contention over multiple ways of framing the practical role, each of which entails a distinctive approach to problem setting and solving. And, when practitioners do resolve conflicting role frames, they do so through a kind of inquiry that falls outside the model of technical rationality.[53]

As Lindblom and Schon wrote, real-world practice limits the utility of a problem-solving approach which relies on the dictates of rational, means-ends analysis. The workday life of professionals, however, is not necessarily based on a random, trial-and-error, fly-by-the-seat-of-the-pants mentality. Rather, it depends on tacit knowing in action. Every competent practitioner can recognize phenomena—families of behavior associated with a particular problem, situations or circumstances that warrant a particular type of intervention—for which he/she cannot give a reasonably accurate or complete description. Yet in day-to-day practice, the practitioner makes innumerable judgments of quality for which he/she cannot state adequate criteria, and she displays skills for which he/she cannot state the rules or procedures. Even when the practitioner makes conscious use of research-based theories, empirically-based evidence or techniques, he/she is dependent on tacit recognitions and judgments. Professional practitioners often think about what they do, oftentimes while doing it. Perhaps surprised, they reflect on action and on the knowledge which is implicit in that action.[54]

As is common in human service organizations, direct service practitioners and managers both find themselves in uncertain or unique situations. In general, they experience surprise, puzzlement or confusion. Practitioners reflect on the phenomena before them, and on the experience and understanding implicit in their behavior. They then carry out an experiment to generate both a new understanding of the phenomenon and a change in the situation; this behavior is more than mere trial by error.[55]

When someone "reflects-in-action," he becomes a researcher in the practice context. He/she is not dependent on the categories of established theory and technique, but constructs a new explanatory framework or theory of that unique case. This inquiry is not limited to deliberation about means depending on prior agreement about ends. Nor does the practitioner keep means and ends separate, but rather defines them interactively as he/she frames a problematic situation. Thinking and doing are linked. Inquiry is built into implementation. Thus, "reflection-in-action" proceeds rigorously, although it is not bound by the dichotomies of technical rationality.[56]

The distinctions between action and decision making based on rationality vis-à-vis reflection-in-action or based on a comprehensive rational vis-à-vis a successive limited comparisons model are drawn for purposes of discussion only. Invariably, the way human service administrators and practitioners make decisions requires construction of a role set which combines different levels of personal and professional skills and different levels of functions and responsibilities. In his examination of the role of social service administrators, for example, Wilson suggests there are specific attributes associated with personal skill and with level of institutional functioning. Table 3.4 summarizes these skills and functional levels.

The complex of skills and tasks presented in Table 3.4 are examples of demands which can be placed on any practicing social services administrator. The technical and value-related components are developed in an interrelated fashion, and not as separable elements. Agency goals are abstract concepts derived from societal values, for example, stated as measurable outcome objectives through which the relative attainment of goals can be documented. To the extent a management information system is seen not just as a means for exerting managerial control but as a

Table 3.4.

Examples of Administrative Levels of Skills and Monitoring

Levels	Personal Skill Areas		
	Conceptual	Technical	Interpersonal
Institutional Level	Relate agency's goals to broader social goals, indicators Identify external conditions which will mandate agency accountability	Awareness of legislative judicial, executive policy Financial and social trend analysis abilities	Build political support for agency goals Personify agency goals, in terms of personal practice
	Conceive of advocacy system, viewed partly as an accountability mechanism	Ability to analyze accountability trends	Motivate staff, client and community involvement in system
		Structure, build advocacy system	Promote staff openness to externally evolving standards
		Relate standards to practice realities	

89

Table 3.4 (continued)

Examples of Administrative Levels of Skills and Monitoring

Personal Skill Areas

Levels	Conceptual	Technical	Interpersonal
Managerial Level	Guide agency's social problem definition consistent with its goals and practice capacities	Analyze impacts of alternative types of problem statement	Involve Board staff in defining problems. Maintain reward system consistent with managerial and people needs
	Rationalize the administrative decision making process	Oversee design and management of financial management procedures	Motivate and organize staff and other inputs into MBO system
	Identify decision criteria whereby internally motivated change is required	Oversee design and management of management information system	Involve agency system actors in dealing with financial issues, in sharing managerial responsibility
	Identify planning and communications systems to be used for accountability objectives	Create mechanisms for generation of management objectives in agency	

90

Table 3.4 (continued)

Examples of Administrative Levels of Skills and Monitoring

Levels	Personal Skill Areas		
	Conceptual	Technical	Interpersonal
Technical Level	Oversee operationalization of goals into measurable objectives	Understanding of direct and indirect indicators of client progress	Involve staff, clients in defining measurable objectives
	Identify technical staff competencies needed and necessity of reliance on outside resources	Select viable technical means for maintaining accountability	Support staff in building technical competence into practice roles
		Promote design and maintenance of a practice monitoring information system	Motivate involvement in personnel and peer review systems

Source: Adapted from Scott Muir Wilson, "Values and Technology: Foundations for Practice," in Leadership in Social Administration, ed. by Felice Davidson Perlmutter and Simon Slavin (Philadelphia: Temple University Press, 1980), pp. 112-13.

way of identifying staff and client-defined data needs, it relates to both practice and advocacy concerns.[57]

Although this complex of skills and tasks seems rational, it also suggests that the administrator qua practitioner faces problems on different levels which require distinct, but interrelated, skills. Thus, the administrator brings a range of conceptual, technical and interpersonal skills to a variety of problems. Furthermore, if one were to roughly equate the three levels of functioning (institutional, managerial and technical) with the immediacy of decision making at each level, it becomes clear, on the whole, there is less immediacy associated with the institutional level than at the technical level. Thus, although highly influenced by political factors, institutional-level decisions over time can take into account rational factors while decisions at the technical level, based on an accumulation of rationally attained expertise, can occur on such short notice that deliberation and calculation are at a minimum.

On the whole, managerial and direct service functions in human service organizations contain some aspects which can be construed as rational, albeit in a limited sense, and other aspects which might best be construed as "a-rational," beyond the political. Decisions, for example, based upon successive limited comparisons of one's past experience to an immediate problem, are only in a narrow sense "rational," and they may have little or nothing to do with political aspects of resource allocations. In any event, the discussion of how managers and direct service practitioners think in action and how they face different levels of decisions highlights the rather limited role information plays in the process of making decisions and taking action. The virtual absence of systematically gathered and analyzed data suggests that "control systems" in human service organizations lack as clear an operational source of accountability as in other types of organizations.

Essentially, systems that control the pace and caliber of work are normal to industry. These control systems perform three functions. They measure some aspect of work; compare the actual level to a desired level; and adjust the work in order to minimize the difference between the actual and desired level. In profit-seeking organizations, the systems performing these functions are called management control systems. Their purpose is to evaluate the effectiveness and efficiency with which managerial plans are carried out. The systems consist of a structure, which measures both actual and expected performance, and a process for adjusting the difference between the two.[58]

As noted previously, it is difficult to measure either inputs or outputs in human service organizations. The measurement of output volume frequently defies the imagination, as any close examination, for example, of a United Way definition of acceptable output and what a provider agency actually includes in its reporting figures. Guidelines are invariably stretched beyond stated limits to keep "the numbers" high and accurate enough for maximum funding. Some managers claim it is difficult to measure output accurately anyway, particularly in quality and, therefore, the measurement process is untenable. Relevant data are conspicuously and consistently absent in human service organizations, despite the vast accumulation and processing of routinely gathered data. Even when data are available, it is questionable whether or not and to what extent, they would be used for control. Most human service organizations, as noted earlier, are managed by professionals. Their professional training stressed peer respect, group interdependency and professional competence. These norms are antithetical to the hierarchical, corporate version of the control process. Thus, managers of human service organizations are both professionally and politically resistant to installing accurate output measurement systems.[59]

Furthermore, there is much confusion in the language of human service managers over such terms as "effect," "effectiveness," "efficiency" and "accountability." Each of these in itself relies on some use of information to derive its meaning. Effectiveness is measured by comparing criteria associated with terminal values against achievement of goals. As noted above, these terminal values are often lacking in the human services or else stretched so broadly to achieve consensus they become meaningless. Effect, on the other hand, is measured in relation to criteria derived from purposes associated with instrumental values. In light of the indefinite methods characteristic to human service organizations, even the instrumental effects of a specified procedure or service complicates measurement.[60]

Efficiency implies the best use of resources and methods to achieve goals and purposes; it relies more on the formulation of managerial practice principles to guide political and economic judgments. And, finally, accountability poses the question "Answerable for one's actions and decisions to whom?" Here again, mechanisms and techniques for assuring accountability differ with the interests of those for whom the results are intended. Consumers, funding sources, the community, the profession, one's superiors and also oneself, have different interests in and standards for service decisions. Essential are not measurements, but a set of guiding principles to illuminate the method so as to assure a just and fair, not merely convenient, response to requests for accountability.[61]

The management control function takes into account effectiveness and effect as well as efficiency and accountability. This means human service control functions rest on both rational and political methods for making decisions, particularly decisions about the distribution or allocation of resources. In this, control may be construed as synonymous with power, and the control structure or system of an organization is another way of thinking about the distribution of power and authority within the organization. In a sense, power is based on control of resources and authority, particularly in its formal sense, is the responsibilities and duties commensurate with the control over specified resources. Gummer argues that the structure of an organization at any given time is best seen as the product of the most recent struggle for power among organization subunits, with the winner (being the unit able to establish control over resources) establishing the agenda for organizational analysis.[62]

The nature and dynamics characteristic of human service management and provision of services ordinarily cause little use of systematically gathered and scrutinized information. With the role of information and use of information systems becoming more and more predominant in contemporary society, the idea of information as a resource, like time and money, takes on additional significance. Even human service organizations are likely to undergo a crisis over presumably accepted values, if not a sweeping realignment of power bases and authority structures during the introduction of computer technology and information systems because they accentuate the importance of information decision-making processes.

SUMMARY

Some aspects of human service organizations make the introduction of information systems a major cause of concern. By and large, ideological principles guide service procedures which differ from the rational criteria guiding information management. Human service methods are moral systems with indeterminate linkages between intervention and outcomes, grounded in competitive ideologies, relying on face-to-face interactions and requiring client cooperation. These attributes are common to people-processing, people-sustaining and people-changing systems.

Although rationality pervades these systems, other, nonrational elements dominate human service organizations and service delivery. They face turbulent environments characterized by multiple, often conflicting goals. Their systems incorporate many ill-defined tasks and activities which vary widely among organizations and practitioners. They are difficult to monitor and evaluate. And, most client-staff encounters, the predominant activity in human service organizations, are not readily subject to organizational control.

In human service organizations, the tension between direct service professionals and administrators become particularly acute. By and large, professional power and authority are manifested through the ability of the profession to determine and control conditions of their work and to attain autonomy from organizational evaluation and administrative authority. On the whole, administrators and supervisors in human service organizations judge and evaluate their colleagues on the basis of both agency and professional goals. Conflicting demands further compound management and decision making as well as the use of information in human service organizations.

In most human service organizations, collection and use of information are basically informal, rather than systematic, goal-directed processes, intended primarily for meeting funding requirements. In addition, decision making is far from routine or rational. Most decision making is heavily influenced, if not determined, by political and value-oriented factors, often oriented toward several competing objectives simultaneously. Neither administrators nor practitioners resolve problems following the dictates of technical rationality. As Lindblom and Schon noted, the demands of real-world practice limit the usefulness of an approach to problem solving which relies on the dictates of rational, means-ends calculations.

Tables 3.3 and 3.4 helped to illustrate that, on the whole, managerial and direct service functions in human service organizations contain some aspects that can be seen as rational, albeit in a limited sense, and other aspects that might best be viewed as "a rational," intended to be more than political. In such an environment, the management control function becomes highly problematic, particularly in light of the difficulty of measuring outcomes and of the ambiguity surrounding such terms as effectiveness, efficiency, accountability and effect. The control function invariably rests on both rational and political criteria for making decisions. In human service organizations, guided as they are by ideologies, the political dimension eclipses the rational. The relatively recent demand for accountability from both the public and private sectors resulted, in part, in attempts to tip the balance in favor of the rational. The introduction of computer technology and information systems into human services accentuates the importance of rationality and information in the decision-making process.

NOTES

1. Herbert D. Stein, *Organization and the Human Services: Cross-Disciplinary Reflections* (Philadelphia: Temple University Press, 1981), pp. 45-5.

2. John E. Tropman, *Policy Management in the Human Services* (New York: Columbia University Press, 1984), pp. 36-37.

3. Rino J. Patti, "Social Work Practice Organizational Environment," in *Change from Within: Humanizing Social Welfare Organizations*, ed. by Herman Resnick & Rino J. Patti (Philadelphia: Temple University Press, 1980), pp. 46-56; Herbert D. Stein, "The Concept of Human Service Organization: A Critique" in *Organization and the Human Services,* pp. 24-36.

4. The following four points are taken from Rosemary C. Sarri & Yeheskel Hasenfeld (eds.), *The Management of Human Services* (New York: Columbia University Press, 1978), pp. 2-5. Sarri and Hasenfeld note that whether one conceptualizes human service organizations as a distinct and unique set of organizations depends on the importance attached to these four attributes which characterize them.

5. Charles Perrow, "Hospitals: Technology, Structure and Goals" in *Handbook of Organizations*, ed. by J. G. March (Chicago: Rand McNally, 1965), pp. 910-71.

6. For example, see S. P. Segal, "Research in the Outcome of Social Work Therapeutic Intervention," *Journal of Health and Social Behavior*, 13 (March, 1972): 3-17.

7. Edward Newman & Jerry Turem, "The Crisis of Accountability," *Social Work*, 19 (January, 1974): 5-16.

8. Robert N. Anthony & Regina E. Herzlinger, *Management Control in Nonprofit Organizations* (Homewood, IL: Richard D. Irwin, 1975), pp. 1-9.

9. The following is a summary of what appears in Yeheskel Hasenfeld, *Human Service Organizations* (Englewood Cliffs, NJ: Prentice-Hall, 1983), pp. 115-124.

10. R. Rapoport, *Community as a Doctor* (London: Tavistock, 1960), p. 269.

11. Hasenfeld, *Human Service Organizations*, p. 119.

12. B. Lerner & D. W. Fisk, "Client Attributes and the Eyes of the Beholder," *Journal of Consulting and Clinical Psychology*, 40 (1973): 272-77.

13. Hasenfeld, *Human Service Organizations*, p. 120.

14. Ibid., p. 121; Michael Lipsky, *Street-Level Bureaucracy* (New York: Russell Sage Foundation, 1980).

15. Hasenfeld, *Human Service Organizations*, p. 122.

16. Ibid., p. 123.

17. Ibid., pp. 134-43.

18. Ibid., pp. 140-43.

19. A good portion of this literature was covered in Chapter 1. See also

James D. Thompson, *Organizations in Action* (New York: McGraw-Hill, 1967); J. Hage & M. Aikin, "Routine Technology, Social Structure and Organizational Goals," *Administrative Science Quarterly*, 14 (September, 1969): 366-77 and "Relationship of Centralization to Other Structural Properties," *Administrative Science Quarterly*, 12 (November, 1967): 72-91; and Peter M. Blau & R. Schoenherr, *The Structure of Organizations* (New York: Basic Books, 1971).

20. Hasenfeld, *Human Service Organizations*, pp. 148-49.

21. Ibid., p. 159.

22. C. R. Hinings et al., "Structural Conditions of Intraorganizational Power," *Administrative Science Quarterly*, 19 (November, 1974): 22-44.

23. J. Lorber & R. Satow, "Creating a Company of Equals: Sources of Occupational Stratification in a Ghetto Community Mental Health Center," *Sociology of Work and Occupations*, 4 (August, 1977): 281-302.

24. Hasenfeld, *Human Service Organizations*, p. 159.

25. Ibid., p. 160; M. N. Zald, "Organizational Control Structures in Five Correctional Institutions," *American Journal of Sociology*, 68 (November, 1962): 335-45.

26. Hasenfeld, op. cit., pp. 160-61.

27. For example, see A. S. Tannenbaum, *Hierarchy in Organizations* (San Francisco: Jossey-Bass, 1974).

28. G. Zeitz, "Hierarchical Authority and Decision Making in Professional Organizations," *Administration and Society*, 12 (November, 1980): 277-300.

29. Robert L. Peabody, *Organizational Authority* (New York: Atherton Press, 1964).

30. Smith, "Front-Line Organization of the State Mental Hospital."

31. J. M. Prottas, *People-Processing* (Lexington, MA: D. C. Heath, 1979); Hasenfeld, *Human Service Organizations*, pp. 161-62.

32. L. B. Nilson, "The Application of the Occupational 'Uncertainty' Principle to the Professions," *Social Problems*, 26 (June, 1979): 570-81.

33. E. Freidson, *Profession of Medicine* (New York: Dodd, Mead Co., 1970) and T. Johnson, *Professions and Power* (London: Macmillan, 1972).

34. Hasenfeld, *Human Service Organizations*, p. 162.

35. See also, Richard H. Hall, "Professionalization and Bureaucratization," *American Sociological Review*, 33 (February, 1968): 92-104.

36. Hasenfeld, *Human Service Organizations*, pp. 163-64.

37. M. Goss, "Patterns of Bureaucracy Among Hospital Staff Physicians," in *The Hospital in Modern Society*, ed. by E. Freidson (New York: The Free Press, 1963), pp. 170-94.

38. S. K. Ruzek, "Making Social Work Accountable," in *The Professions and Their Prospects*, ed. by E. Freidson (Beverly Hills, CA: Sage, 1973), pp. 217-43. Quote appears in Hasenfeld, *Human Service Organizations*, p. 164.

39. Myron E. Weiner, *Human Services Management: Analysis and Applications* (Homewood, IL: Dorsey Press, 1982), p. 7.

40. Michael D. Cohen, James G. March & Johan P. Olsen, "A Garbage Can Model of Organizational Choice," *Administration Science Quarterly*, 17 (March, 1972): 1-25.

41. Burton Gummer, "Organization Theory for Social Administration," in *Leadership in Social Administration: Perspectives for the 1980s*, ed. by Felice Davidson Perlmutter & Simon Slavin (Philadelphia: Temple University Press, 1980), pp. 22-49.

42. Thomas P. Holland, "Information and Decision Making in Human Services, *Administration in Mental Health*, 4 (Fall, 1976): 27-28.

43. Cohen et al., "A Garbage Can Model of Organizational Choice," p. 2.

44. Holland, "Information and Decision Making in Human Services," p. 29.

45. Ibid., p. 29.

46. Ibid., p. 31.

47. Ibid., p. 33.

48. Charles E. Lindblom, "The Science of 'Muddling Through'," *Public Administration Review*, 19 (Spring, 1959): 79-88.

49. Chris Argyris, "Some Limits of Rational Man Organizational Theory," *Public Administration Review*, 33 (May/June, 1973): 253-67.

50. Donald A. Schon, *The Reflective Practitioner: How Professionals Think in Action* (New York: Basic Books, 1983).

51. For example, see Richard J. Bernstein, *The Restructuring of Social and Political Theory* (New York: Harcourt Brace Jovanovich, 1976).

52. Cohen et al., "A Garbage Can Model of Organizational Choice," pp. 1-3.

53. Schon, *The Reflective Practitioner*, pp. 37-48.

54. Ibid., pp. 49-50.

55. Ibid., p. 68.

56. Ibid., pp. 68-69.

57. Scott Muir Wilson, "Values and Technology: Foundations for Practice" in *Leadership in Social Administration*, ed. by Davidson & Slavin, pp. 111-12.

58. Regina E. Herzlinger, "Management Control Systems in Human Service Organizations" in *Organization and the Human Services*, ed. by Stein, p. 205.

59. Ibid., p. 209.

60. Harold Lewis, "Management in the Nonprofit Social Service Organization," *Child Welfare*, 54 (November, 1975): 620.

61. Ibid., pp. 621-22.

62. Gummer, "Organizational Theory for Social Administration," pp. 42-43.

Chapter 4

Information Systems
and the Human Service
Organization

Despite the differences between human service organizations and other types of organizations, particularly those for profit, the past 35 years' growth of business data processing (DP) foreshadows things to come to human service organizations as their use of DP increases in the coming decades. Human services will manage data by purchasing DP technologies and developing information systems that business took years to develop. The DP system is defined as all automated data collection, storage, manipulation, retrieval and reporting in the operation and management of an organization. And, as did many a business, a human service agency must go through the long, tedious and frustrating process of adapting a DP system to the organization and the user if it is to be successful.[1]

The business use and growth of data processing and information systems can be useful to examine since this can point to some difficulties human service agencies are likely to experience, particularly those of the distribution of authority and the decision load. Concomitantly, a brief look at computer technology as currently used in human services provides background for assessing the impact of the implementation of information systems on the distribution of authority and the decision load.

THE DEVELOPMENT AND USE
OF COMPUTER TECHNOLOGY
AND INFORMATION SYSTEMS

Stages of Development

Schoech and Schkade identify six steps in the development of organizational data processing: initiation, extension, modification, integration, data administration and maturity. In initiation, there is automation of several low-level operating systems in a function, typically accounting, in which DP personnel have specialized technological learning and there is lax planning and control. During extension, automation expands into other operational functions and emphasizes user-oriented applications. In the third stage, modification, emphasis shifts from managing the computer to managing the data. Documentation is more complete and existing applications are redesigned to put the DP function at the middle management level.[2]

In the later stages of development, DP broadens its scope to that of information systems (IS) proper, which entails increased legitimacy of IS, to the point of having functional management responsibilities just as personnel and accounting. In the fourth stage of organizational data processing, integration, existing applications are again retrofitted, using data-base technology, and the system grows rapidly moving out to the user. Rapid growth signals the fifth stage, data administration, where the data processing function is moved higher in the organization, and there is some integration of applications through shared data and common systems. The system matures and mirrors the organization's data flow. The mature IS function focuses on data resource management and data resource strategic planning. There is joint accountability between user and data processing, in which IS staff have functional responsibilities with other units.[3]

The growth stages of human services data processing can be compared to those of DP in business. Figure 4.1 highlights those trends. The important factor to note in Figure 4.1 is that the pattern of growth of human services computerized data processing is

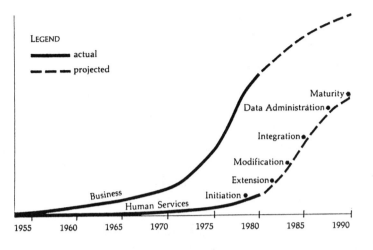

Note: Growth rate is based on total calculations and data manipulations.

Figure 4.1: Comparison of Data Processing Growth in Business and Human Services. (Adapted from Dick J. Schoech and Lawrence L. Schkade, "What Human Services Can Learn from Business About Computerization," *Public Welfare*, 38 [Summer, 1980]: 22.)

projected roughly to parallel the previously recorded growth in business. Several factors, however, may retard that rate of development. First, it is very difficult to develop standardized measurable units of service for defining human services inputs and outputs and the impact these have on clients. Second, collecting service data across agency boundaries is extremely difficult because the political and territorial nature of the diverse delivery "system." And, third, although human service organizations can buy technologies in moving from the initiation stage to that of modification or integration, movement beyond that to the stages of data administration and maturity require considerable learning and adaptation on the part of the agency. In the latter stages, changes cannot be rushed, particularly since organizational acceptance of IS with functional managerial responsibilities invariably entails conflicts over structural authority. The information system must be revised and adapted until it fits the organization. This process requires changes both in ways of thinking about organizational structures and functional relationships with other departments or programs.[4]

Use of Computer Technology in Human Services

To determine the actual use of computers and the level of development of information systems is problematic. Because human service agency experience of has not been as extensive as that of business and local government, there is simply less information available. Studies in the late 1970s found the use of computers in human service organizations primarily limited to the budgeting process.[5] More recently, a 1984 survey of human service agencies revealed that about 30% of public agencies (137 of 460) and 40% of private agencies (132 of 336) were using microcomputers. The lower rate of use public agencies reported reflects, in part, their use of larger mainframe computers and minicomputers not covered in the survey.[6]

In a review of nine social work journals from 1970 through 1976, Boyd, Hylton and Price found 31 articles on the use of computer applications in human services. The authors concluded that computers "in social welfare settings have been used almost exclusively for clerical work, record keeping and accounting. . . ."[7] In the 1984 survey mentioned above, uses were almost exclusively for word processing, spread sheets and data management. Accounting and statistics, the more traditional computer uses, fared poorly by comparison in this survey.[8] A 1984 survey of Family Service America agencies on microcomputer use corroborated these findings.[9]

Computer use as a potential tool for the direct-service worker was unrecognized in the professional literature before 1980. Sparse attention was given to incorporating computer training in the education of professional social workers.[10] In the 1980s, however, there has been a marked increase in the computer applications in both direct practice and administration, particularly for purposes other than accountability, namely planning and decision making. Nurius and Mutschler, for example, describe changes in the master's program of the University of Michigan School of Social Work which address training gaps in utilization of computer-assisted information and evaluation systems.[11] The School of Social Service Administration at The University of Chicago has integrated courses on information systems into its management sequence.

The field of public welfare has made use of automated information systems for purposes of administration and planning.[12] Such systems as CYCIS, a child welfare and youth services system, and PROSYS, a national model information system for adult probation, are indicative of large scale uses of automated information systems. The National Opinion Research Center has assisted the Illinois Department of Children and Family Services in using information routinely gathered and stored for purposes of planning and policy formation.[13] Schwartz has compiled a rather comprehensive set of papers touching all aspects of computer use in clinical mental health settings.[14] And, finally, the editors of *Administration in Social Work* devoted a special issue to the application of computers in social service and mental health agencies.[15] It is finally clear that automation has permeated human services.

ASSESSING THE IMPACT
OF AUTOMATED INFORMATION SYSTEMS
ON BUREAUCRATIC STRUCTURE

Overview

Automation, as an organizational phenomenon, is extremely important because it can change fundamental administrative processes. Human relations research on automation assumes that the impact of automation on the worker is direct, not mediated by formal organizational structure, such as the hierarchy of authority, division of labor, rules, regulations and the like. Myer, however, rejects that assumption and demonstrates how the use of a computer and its concomitant data processing embellishment and expansion or elevation of information systems functions change the administrative structure of organizations.[16]

Where the data processing function sits in a bureaucracy has important effects on administrative processes. Most automated organizations have data processing and information systems management staff whose work is not a primary goal of these organizations. Essentially, the data processing staff is composed of specialists, whose work is not understood by others, who perform a service for other units of organization. The formation of a data processing staff of specialists in an organization creates interdependence to a degree greater than prior to its introduction. Various line units, whose activities contribute directly to organizational goals, must rely on the performance of data processing staff to accomplish their goals.[17]

This interdependence of line units and data processing staff requires horizontal communication between them. If no changes are made in traditional forms of organization, high-status members of line units must deal with low-status data processing experts. Most frequently, the "clients" of data processing staff are heads of line units or their assistants. Nonsupervisory line personnel generally have little to do with data processing, and, despite some of the clinical uses of automation, there are those who remain at best cautious and, if not, are quite skeptical.[18] The head of a line division has high status in the organization, but, chances are, she understands little of what the computer, data processing staff and, in many instances, the data processing and information systems functions can and cannot do for her. In such cases, the high-level line supervisor who has a low-level of expertise about computers relates to low-level data processing staff who have high level technical expertise. Disagreements and tensions are likely to ensue, particularly if and when higher level supervisory staff assert the authority of their office to accomplish tasks lower-level technical staff deem unreasonable.[19]

In a study of 254 city, county and state departments of finance or comptrollers' offices, Meyer found a proliferation of supervisory levels in data processing divisions. Further, they less often required personnel to hold a college degree: 19.5% of positions were degreed, compared to 25.9% in nonautomated departments and 29.9% in line divisions of automated departments. College-trained personnel unevenly distributed between data processing staff and line division staff in any organization exacerbates the difficulties caused by interdependence. Therefore, higher-level supervisory positions, requiring higher educational levels and other professional skills, are created to ensure that high-status members of line divisions deal only with a high-status, more highly educated member of the data processing unit.[20]

Meyer suggests that automation increases the interdependence between the data processing units of an organization and those divisions relying on information generated by these units. As interdependence deepens, there are organizational changes. Structurally, more highly educated IS staff come to occupy higher status positions in an organization, thereby achieving structural parity with higher status administrative staff of other departments, interacting with them accordingly. Functionally, IS staff become increasingly involved in all aspects of organization which generate or require information, direct-service programs as well as accounting and finance. This two-pronged interdependence creates difficulties in organizations with older, traditional, hierarchical structures, and a rigid chain of command resting on vertical channels of communication. On the other hand, organizations that have dispensed, at least in part, with vertical patterns of communication and that allow horizontal interchange reduce the difficulties and tensions caused by automation's increased interdependence.

Organizational Structure and Management Information Systems Department

The experience of business has been that implementation and use of data processing and information systems are severely limited if the person in charge of the data processing division or unit reports to anyone two levels or more below the chief executive.[21] In early stages of development, data processing and information systems functions are placed in the department of first application, usually accounting or finance. Separate, high-level units are created only when the first applications proves viable. Such development, however, conceals a serious trap. Gibson and Nolan, for example, note that the department controlling information as a resource becomes strongly protective of it, often because a manager or group within the department wants to build up power and influence.[22] As the data processing function assumes a broader role in the organization, which happens over time, conflict arises between higher-level staff of information system units and the higher-level supervisory staff of other functional areas. The growth of data processing and information systems requires an organization's information to be considered a core resource and its data processing system a model of the organization's structure, processes and procedures.[23] Hence, one of the more intriguing questions on organizational structure associated with management information systems is "where should the MIS department be located?"[24]

Here again, the experience of business can benefit our knowledge of the issue. Essentially, as the technology "advanced," the structural position of electronic data processing functions also changed. At the risk of oversimplification, each of the four generations of computer technology was accompanied by changes in the MIS department location.

First, because early computers were recognized chiefly for their prodigious arithmetic skills, managers generally associated computer applications with accounting activities and located their data processing activity within the accounting department. As the second generation of computers become available and as computer applications were developed for production, personnel, marketing and other functions, several departments and divisions acquired computers and the personnel to operate and program them. This occurred often because second-generation computers could not accommodate all demand for storage (memory) and processing (CPU). The third generation of computer technology provided capacity to handle all organizational applications, though primarily in a centralized manner, through remote terminals at many organization locations with easy access to the central mainframe computer. In many organizations, a new high-level department was created to control and coordinate information system activities for the functional departments, and, perhaps most important, to provide functionally integrated management information to top-level decision makers.[25]

Human service organizations now are entering an era of computer usage, at a time when they face the rather conflicting focus peculiar to the fourth generation of computer hardware and software. On the one hand, fourth-generation computers have enormous capacity, remote data entry is easy and organization-wide data base management systems are increasingly used; these all suggest use of a centralized system, where the higher the control is placed in the organization, the better. On the other hand, low cost minicomputers, which blend second-generation capacity with other considerations, such as ease of operation, reduced maintenance and environmental controls, with third or fourth-generation technology, seem to favor decentralization. Furthermore, the range of MIS-related skills and activities has broadened and spread to such an extent that personnel throughout an organization are now capable of performing tasks once the responsibility of a few elite specialists.[26]

Once again, the experience in business highlights some problems human service organizations will encounter as they develop information systems. During the 1960s, a trend began to locate electronic data processing and information systems outside the traditional accounting departments.[27] But, even in the late 1960s, finance and accounting departments still housed the majority of information systems departments.[28] By 1976, however, a study of 150 randomly selected large business and government organizations showed that only a third of units with information system responsibility still reported to the finance or accounting departments.[29] Location depended upon industrial category. For example, financial institutions, among the earliest commercial users of computers, were also among the first to create separate information systems departments. And, in government organizations, 61.5% had separate departments of information systems compared to the 7.2% in which IS remained in departments of accounting or finance.

The creation of separate departments of information systems seems to increase the potential for tension surrounding interdepartmental relations and communication patterns. Most human service organizations with an MIS separate function from others less than industry and business. Invariably, it is linked to other functions such as departments of planning, research or quality assurance, insuring information systems cannot yet achieve parity with other functional units. Still perceived as an administrative adjunct, interrelations with other staff are subordinate rather than complementary to their needs.

To the extent the MIS function is separate, its supervisory and administrative staff advise, consult and even guide other functional departments' higher-level staff as well as the agency or organization's administrative and executive staff, because direct service administrators and supervisors are generally ignorant about computer technology and information systems. In those environments with separate MIS departments, IS management is perceived as legitimate in its own right, much like the shared human resources management responsibilities of personnel and accounting. Although jurisdictional issues still abound, the MIS department can claim its own functional management arena, which includes influencing the role information plays in decision making.

On the whole, it should be noted that there is no single best MIS location. Although placing it at a high level in the organization demonstrates management's commitment to the MIS function and the importance of information as an integral resource to decision making, the changes caused by introducing and implementing MIS in human service organizations may offset the intended advantages. In sum, the technology and uses of the MIS are not neutral. They affect the organization's cultural and political climates in ways that raise legitimate questions as well as irrational resistances or fears.[30] Thus, it is important to consider how the MIS function is itself structured and how it interacts with other functional areas in the organization.

THE IMPACT OF MIS
IN HUMAN SERVICE ORGANIZATIONS

Management and Information Technology

In 1958, Harold Leavitt and Thomas Whisler forecasted changes the new information technology would have on management in the 1980s. They predicted information technology would have its greatest impact on middle and top management and lead to opposite conclusions dictated by "participative management," a philosophy then popular. In the 1950s, information technology was at the periphery of management. Its applications were, for the most part, independent of central organizational issues such as communication and creativity. Leavitt and Whisler predicted organizations in the 1980s would be more highly centralized, with top executives less dependent on subordinates whose spheres of judgment and experience would be circumscribed by information technology. There would be fewer middle managers, most of whom would be more routine technicians than thinkers.[31]

From their vantage in the mid-1950s, information technology also promised to eliminate those less than adequate decisions which arise from garbled communications, from misconceptions of goals and from unsatisfactory measurement of the partial contributions of each of dozens of line and staff specialists. In short, 1980s middle management would break into two segments, with the larger taking more highly programmed tasks and the smaller rising to a level where more creative thinking is needed and where the organization locates more authority and responsibility. In this concept, top management would focus more on innovation and change, become more abstract, more search and research-oriented and, correspondingly, less directly involved in the making of routine decisions. Thus, information technology, according to Leavitt and Whisler, would encourage "researchers" or "people like researchers" to be located near the top of the organization hierarchy, thereby influencing the direction of and innovation in the organization.[32] It is doubtful that "people like researchers" moved into top management positions as Leavitt and Whisler posited. Nonetheless, one human service executive has argued for locating the MIS in the research department, assuming, as is true in many human service organizations, an agency cannot support a separate MIS department.[33]

Regardless of location, information technology does foster a rational and comprehensive oriented way of thinking and process of decision making. In a study of 11 firms in the Minneapolis-St. Paul area, for example, Vergin found the use of the computer ". . . enabled a wider view to be taken in decision making . . . which explicitly considered operations throughout large segments of the firm . . ." on the departmental level.[34]

Vergin also found greater organizational revisions in those firms placing more importance on data processing in their total operations. His study corroborated Leavitt and Whisler's predictions of more centralized decision making and downgrading of some middle management positions. It also affirmed that data processing units gained stature in the organizational structure. Essentially, data processing became responsible for designing the information system and, often, given authority to coordinate activities among other functional areas. The data processing unit moved from an obscure, low-level location in the accounting division to independent status under a top-level executive.[35] Since the human services are under increasing pressure to develop accountability and sound management practices, information's role and the MIS department's location in the organizational structure affect the politics and nature of decision making and, thereby, the hierarchy of formal authority.[36]

The increased demand for accountability in human services emphasizes information as a resource and fosters the integration, if not centralization, of the data processing function and, perhaps, of other functional units.[37] Those who control information flow to administrators and other "authorities" in human service organization play a pivotal, almost gatekeeping role. Easton suggests that gatekeepers are generally likely to have the greatest number and variety of interpersonal and organizational contacts and for whom it is possible not only to open and close communication channels but also to collect and reformulate information.[38] Increasingly, the locating the MIS department at higher levels in the organization and the relying on administrators and supervisors with expertise in computer technology for information shifts the structures of power and authority in human service organizations.

Power structures rest less on social consensus between superiors and subordinates about privileges or rights than on distribution of resources and the means by which allocation can be enforced. Erection of the structure entails a process in which the possession and control of system-relevant resources are skillfully used.[39] There is little doubt that information, whether for purposes of accountability or for purposes of decision making, functions more and more like other resources, such as money and manpower. As an essential resource, information places those who control it in a position of power. When this position is at a high level in the organization, its authority is that much greater and its staff can exert control over functional units. Thus, information technology brings the possibility that staff responsible for ensuring an adequate and timely flow of information to those who need it rise to such high-level positions it is also possible for them to influence the direction of other functional units. This is one of the effects information technology has on the structure of authority and the distribution of the decision load in human service organizations.

Authority, Decision Load and the MIS in Human Service Organizations

To date, there is very little information on the organizational changes resulting from an information management application, especially in human services. To the extent human service organizations' MIS experience is parallel to that of business and industry, there are benchmarks to each of the six stages of data processing. Figure 4.2 depicts these benchmarks. Of concern here is the impact certain of these benchmarks have on the authority structure and decision load in human service organizations.

The organization of DP, for example, has moved from a more centralized structure, operating "closed shop," to one in which layers of data processing responsibility exist at appropriate organizational levels. This development is like the development of other industries from a highly skilled, labor-intensive effort to one balanced between centralization with common applications and decentralized user-controlled applications. As the MIS function is increasingly integrated into the organization, it requires changes in who makes what kinds of decisions. Schoech, for example, identifies six major organizational changes in the authority structure of an organization accommodating an integrated MIS application. These changes are as follows:

1. Power shifts to top management, because they get more accurate and timely information.
2. Power shifts to those who understand and use the information management system.
3. Power shifts to those who have linkage and boundary-spanning roles during the implementation process.
4. Decisions become centralized at a higher level in the organization because more accurate data are available to top decision makers and the decisions become complicated by more information.
5. Decision making becomes more structured and less flexible because increased information focuses, quantifies and rationalizes decisions.
6. Sections of the organization become more dependent on each other due to the development, updating and use of a common data base.[40]

The extent of these changes depends on an organization's approach to computer use. With the increased availability of low-

Benchmarks of the Six Stages of Data Processing

First-Level Analysis		Stage 1 Initiation	State 2 Contagion	Stage 3 Control	Stage 4 Integration	Stage 5 Data administration	Stage 6 Maturity
First-Level Analysis	DP expenditure benchmarks	Tracks rate of sales growth	Exceeds rate of sales growth	Is less less than rate of sales growth	Exceeds rate of sales growth	Is less than rate of sales growth	Tracks rate of sales growth
	Technology benchmarks	100% batch processing	80% batch processing	70% batch processing	50% batch and remote job entry processing	20% batch and remote job entry	10% batch and remote job entry processing
			20% remote job entry processing	15% data base processing	40% data base and data communications processing	60% data base and data communications processing	60% data base and data communications processing
				10% inquiry processing	5% personal computing	5% personal computing	5% personal computing
				5% time-sharing processing	5% mini- and micro-computer processing	15% mini- and micro-computer processing	25% mini- and micro-computer processing
Second-Level Analysis	Applications portfolio	Concentration on labor-intensive automation, scientific support, and clerical replacement		Applications move out to user locations for data generation and use		Balance is established between centralized shared data/common system applications and decentralized user-controlled applications	
	DP organization	Data processing is centralized and operates as a "closed shop"		Data processing becomes custodial. Computer utility established, reliable		There is organizational implementation of the data resource management concept	
	DP planning and control	Internal planning and control installed to manage computer. Includes programming standards project management & accountability			External planning and control installed to manage data resources. Includes user charge-back and data administration		
	User awareness	Reactive: superficial user involvement. Better, faster than manual system		Driving force: User directly involved with data entry & use. Held accountable for quality		Participatory: User, data processing accountible for quality and design of relevant applications	

Figure 4.2: Benchmarks of the Six Stages of Data Processing. (From R. L. Nolan, "Managing the Crisis in Data Processing," *Harvard Business Review*, 1979, 57 [2]: 117.)

cost sophisticated computers, there are substantial differences in design. There is the "traditional" mainframe approach to computer and information system design, used for the first two decades of computers and still used for large organizational systems. At the other pole is the relatively new "user-oriented" approach accompanying the technological changes in equipment.[41]

In the traditional approach, specially trained management analysts, computer systems analysts and computer programs accomplished many of the data processing functions, in a unit somewhat separate from other functional units in the organization. In the user-oriented approach, the operating employees, professionals and administrators themselves use the equipment supported by a data system facilitator. In human service organizations, user sophistication remains low compared to that in business and industry, resulting in increasing dependency on technically literate managers and professionals in high-level positions throughout the organization.

At the risk of oversimplification, human service organizations face two basic options directly affecting authority structures and the decision load.

On one hand, computer and information technologies are a highly complex, expensive issue requiring technically trained staff. These staff increase their status and influence in the organization over time as they understand better than others the use of information. This technical elite advise managers in matters which might be construed to belong more appropriately to management. Boundaries between "program" decisions and technical input become blurred. On the other hand, direct user involvement with the information technologies is now possible. The traditional relationship between technology and the user in which the specialist appears as a barrier can more readily be replaced by a new relationship in which the specialist functions as a facilitator. Figure 4.3 illustrates the differences between these approaches.

In either approach, the specialist and the information system intrude upon the organizational structure of authority and on the distribution of the decision load. This involvement invariably en-

Old Relationship   New Relationship

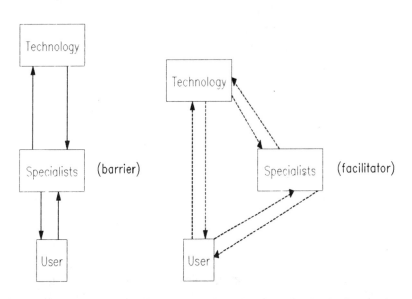

Figure 4.3: Old and New Relationships Between Information Technology and User. (Adapted from Myron E. Weiner, *Human Services Management* [Homewood, IL: Dorsey Press, 1982], pp. 549-50.)

tails a change in the decision load, whose typology appears in Figure 2.1. In the more traditional organizational structure, the MIS personnel serve management by providing information basic to decisions at the policy, organizational, and programmatic levels. As the MIS department assumes a higher position in the organization and as its personnel interact more often with other professional staff, this instrumental aspect of the MIS function diminishes. Instead, the MIS function and its staff increasingly permeate the prerogatives of all levels of management: top, middle and operations. Thus, MIS staff influence all levels of management of the organization, challenging the traditional authority structure.

This challenge to authority within a human service organization comes on three fronts, one structural and two functional. In the structural, the MIS department and its people continue to rise in the organizational hierarchy. The director of this department comes to appear in the organizational chart on the same line as other functional, service department heads. In many human service organizations, this means that the head of the MIS department becomes part of the executive staff. This director takes part in planning for the agency as a whole and influences the organization's direction, as well as the means to get there. In short, the MIS director can come to shape the overall mission of the human service organization or its ends, as well as the steps the organization will need to take to carry out its mission.

In the first of the two functional challenges to authority, MIS brings with it a highly rational, integrative and, to the greatest possible extent, determinant way of thinking about problems. An approach at variance with the indeterminate and ideological aspects of human service organizations (described in detail in the previous chapter). Increased demands for accountability place more and more pressure on human service organizations to demonstrate efficiency and competency. Responses to these demands must rely less on experiential, anecdotal testimonies that any service is inherently good or better than none, but more on systematically rational approaches like MBO, PPBS and task-centered management which purport to improve effectiveness and efficiency.[42]

This increased reliance on rational problem solving challenges the more common intuitive and "art-like" aspects of administrative and clinical practice.[43] These conflicting values produce many problems with information systems in human service agencies. Like human service methods, information systems imply an ideology, a world view containing attitudes and beliefs about the way things are or should be. Based as they are on a systemic approach to problem identification and resolution, these values conflict with those of the social service agency, especially those of professionals, and lead to misunderstandings and resistance.

The further these values pervade the organization, the more legitimacy they have, resulting in the second functional challenge of MIS to authority. When information is seen as a resource like personnel and money, its management requires high-level interactions with other units over a broader scope and at all levels of decision making. As the MIS personnel influence more and more agency-wide decisions, their value system challenges the legitimacy and values of other decision makers.

Weirich identifies four conflicting values: clarity, uniformity, permanency and openness.[44] Implementation of an information system forces increased clarity in organizational characteristics; goals need to be clearly defined and set into measurable objectives. Organizational activities need to be clearly stated and precise indicators of the extent of services must be established. As noted in Chapter 3, however, ambiguity and indeterminacy typify social service organizations. Goals lack clarity and often consist of general value statements. Objectives are difficult to specify and some defy operationalization. Services are difficult to divide into measurable units because many categories overlap.[45]

While clarity is the primary conceptual expectation of an information system, uniformity is the primary behavioral norm, integrating critical aspects of the relatively autonomous services. Standardized language and routine sets of procedures must be employed consistently by all users, data will be unreliable, the system will have little credibility, and the products of the system will be of little use. For the administrator, this means an increased emphasis on organizational control of employee behavior, through rule making, quality control monitoring and enforcement. Human service agencies, however, have high degrees of pluralism and non-conformity. Diversity increases with size of the organization, as the proportion of professionals and the number of speciality units increase. Professional groups and program units develop their own definitions, language and, to some degree, procedures. Attempts to bring these features into a single format suitable to the information system can generate strong resistance.[46]

An information system requires a relatively high degree of organizational stability during its development and implementation. It also needs permanency to be economically run. Human service agencies can be quite unstable. New services and practices emerge in response to community needs and professional developments. Policies change, creating new lines of authority, demanding new forms of data and reshuffling funding sources. The administrator faces a basic dilemma between responsiveness to information needs and responsible information management. Uncontrolled program changes can make information systems useless, while over-protection of the information system can endanger program effectiveness and enforce program rigidity. [47]

Finally, openness presupposes data needed by the system is available and readily given. Although the data base is usually protected from unauthorized entry, human service workers may interpret extensive data collection as an intrusion into their professional domain and a violation of the client-worker relationship, in which the bonds of trust between client and professional are threatened, as are the prerogatives of professional discretion. Professionals may purposely omit or change information, making all information incomplete and unreliable. In addition, privacy within the organization is threatened. The performance of subunits becomes more visible. Without an information system, however, such information automatically goes to others outside the unit, to superiors and funders. To safeguard against any action against it, subunit staff may resist participation or even "fudge" their reports. [48]

The reliance on rational problem solving and decision making undermines the legitimacy accorded to practice wisdom, ideological preference, tradition and professional judgment. Organizational rationality is "bounded" by both internal capacities and external constraints. [49] As noted in previous chapters, decisions are often made on political grounds, for ideological reasons, out of tradition or habit, because of economic feasibility, from intuition or bias, or at times from expediency. Even "reflective practice" mitigates against empirical investigation and rational analysis. Sometimes, "things just seem to happen." Furthermore, administrators use informal networks to acquire information. Although no formal system will replace these qualitative sources, information systems validate making decisions and solving problems on a factual basis, logical connections between means and ends, and expertise. [50]

This pervasive spread of rationality and systemic thinking in the administration of human service agencies encourages manager's attempts to control the precarious nature of human service organizations' environments, the indeterminacy of their methods, and the nonrational aspects of administrative practice. Rationality eclipses judgment. The proliferation of information systems and that world view threaten to displace time-tested practices with the aura of scientific rigor and rational thought. This displacement may prove cost efficient; but the thrust of rational methodologies has been so great in the 20th century that even ends themselves may become blurred. This possibility precipitates an examination of the influence of rational and technocratic thought not only on the functioning of human service organizations, but also on society and social welfare in general.

SUMMARY

The development, use and impact of computer technology and information systems in the human services roughly parallels the previously recorded growth of DP in business. Recent surveys and articles about human service computer use and information systems indicate pervasive acceptance for administration and potential for direct practice, in addition to the more accustomed applications of payroll and finance.

The impact of automated information systems on organizational structure in general and in the human services environment in particular increase in the interdependence between data processing units and the departments relying on the information generated. As IS staff is more highly educated, it comes to occupy higher status positions, achieving structured parity with higher level administrative staff of other departments. IS staff also become more functionally involved in aspects of organization that require information be systematically collected and manipulated. The location of the MIS department was seen as an indicator of the extent to which the IS management function achieved legitimacy in its own right.

The increased demand for accountability in the human services elevates the importance of information as a resource and fosters the integration, if not centralization, of at least the data processing function and perhaps of other functional units. Locating the MIS department in higher levels of the organization and the relying on administrators and supervisors with expertise in computer technology shift the structure of power and authority in human service organizations.

Essentially, power shifts to top management, to those who understand and use the IS system and to those who occupy boundary-spanning roles during the IS implementation process. Additionally, decisions become more centralized and structured, not only in the areas of operations and operational control, but also management control and, to a lesser extent, strategic planning. MIS staff come to occupy higher levels of authority structurally and they influence the management of the organization at all levels functionally, thereby challenging the traditional authority structure.

This challenge occurs on three fronts, one structural and two functional. In the structural, the higher level responsibility of the MIS director enables her to participate in planning for the organization as a whole, which influences the direction the agency takes as well as the means to get there.

There are two functional challenges. The first is that the highly rational, integrative and determinant "world view" endemic to MIS is at variance with the indeterminate and ideological aspects of human service organizations. Technical rationality is seen as preferable to practice wisdom and precedent as a basis for making decisions. Secondly, the role of the MIS function becomes legitimately on par with other functional units. Information is seen as a resource like personnel and money. Its management necessitates high-level interactions among other functional units and over a broader scope of decisions. As the MIS personnel influence more and more agency-wide decisions, their value system challenges the legitimacy and values of other decision makers. Four such values, clarity, uniformity, permanency and openness, when examined, show the probable conflict between the needs of MIS staff and the realities of practitioners.

The proliferation of information systems and that world view in the human services threatens to displace time-tested and reflect practices with those based on the aura of scientific rigor and rational thought. Such a displacement may prove cost efficient. It may nonetheless raise questions about the use of such means to obtain desired ends.

NOTES

1. Dick J. Schoech & Lawrence L. Schkade, "What Human Services Can Learn From Business About Computerization," *Public Welfare*, 38 (Summer, 1980): 18.

2. Ibid., p. 21.

3. Ibid.

4. Ibid., p. 22.

5. United Way of America, *Directory-Data Processing Activity*, Report of the Data Processing Service Committee (Alexandria, VA: June, 1977), p. i; Dick Schoech, *Computer Use in Human Services* (New York: Human Sciences Press, 1982), p. 181.

6. Joseph A. Doucette (ed.), *A Directory of Microcomputer Software in the Human Services* (Portland, ME: Computer Consulting and Programming Associates, 1985), p. 175.

7. Lawrence H. Boyd et al., "Computers in Social Work Practice: A Review, " *Social Work*, 23 (September, 1978): 370. The journals examined were *Social Work, Child Welfare, Journal of Education for Social Work, Social Casework, Social Service Review, Social Policy, Social Issues*, and *Journal of Sociology and Social Welfare*.

8. Doucette, *A Directory of Microcomputer Software in the Human Services*, p. 177.

9. Of the respondents, 88% used microcomputers for word processing, 70% for data base management, 61% for spread sheets and 52% for accounting. There was no formal report of survey results. Raw data were supplied by William B. McCurdy, Family Service America, New York.

10. Boyd et al., "Computers in Social Work Practice: A Review." For one example, however, see Martin Bloom, "Information Science in the Education of Social Work Students," *Journal of Education in Social Work*, 11 (Winter, 1975): 30-35.

11. Paula S. Nurius & Elizabeth Mutschler, "Use of Computer-Assisted Information Processing in Social Work Practice," *Journal of Education for Social Work*, 20 (Winter, 1984): 83-94.

12. Samuel P. Bauer, "The Impact of Automation on Public Welfare Sys-

tems," *Public Welfare*, 31 (Winter, 1973): 39-42; and Eleanor Chelinsky, "Welfare Administration and the Possibilities for Automation," *Public Welfare*, 31 (Summer, 1973): 7-15.

13. Fred Wulczyn, "Administrative Data: Polishing a Tarnished Image," Paper presented at Evaluation '84, The Joint Conference of the Evaluation Research Society and Evaluation Network, San Francisco, CA: November, 1984 (Chicago: Children's Policy Research Project, Social Policy Research Center, NORC and School of Social Service Administration, University of Chicago, October, 1984).

14. Marc D. Schwartz (ed.), *Using Computers in Clinical Practice: Psychotherapy and Mental Health Applications* (New York: Haworth Press, 1984).

15. *Administration in Social Work*, 5 (Fall/Winter, 1981).

16. Marshall W. Meyer, "Automation and Bureaucratic Structure," *American Journal of Sociology*, 74 (November, 1968): 256-64.

17. Ibid., pp. 257-58.

18. For example, see Paul Abels, "Can Computers do Social Work?" *Social Work*, 17 (September, 1972): 5-11.

19. Meyer, "Automation and Bureaucratic Structure," pp. 259-60.

20. Ibid., pp. 260-63.

21. Philip Ein-Dor & Eli Segev, "Organizational Context and the Success of Management Information Systems," *Management Science*, 24 (June, 1978): 1067.

22. Cyrus F. Gibson & Richard L. Nolan, "Managing the Four Stages of EDP Growth," *Harvard Business Review*, 52 (January/February, 1974): 80.

23. Schoech & Schkade, "What Human Services Can Learn from Businesses About Computerization," p. 27.

24. Donald W. Kroeber & Hugh J. Watson, "Is There a Best MIS Department?" *Information and Management*, 2 (October, 1979): 165-73.

25. Ibid., pp. 165-66.

26. Ibid., p. 167.

27. W. E. Rief & R. M. Monczka, "Locating the Systems Department," *Journal of Systems Management*, 24 (December, 1973):

28. Donald W. Kroeber, "An Empirical Study of the Current State of Information Systems Evolution" (Unpublished doctoral dissertation, University of Georgia, Athens, 1976).

29. Kroeber and Watson, "Is There a Best MIS Department Location?" p. 168.

30. Richard K. Caputo, "The Role of Information Systems in Evaluation Research," *Administration in Social Work* (Spring, 1986): 67-77.

31. Harold J. Leavitt & Thomas L. Whisler, "Management in the 1980s," *Harvard Business Review*, 36 (November-December, 1958): 41-44.

32. Ibid., pp. 45-46.

33. Caputo, "The Role of Information Systems in Evaluation Research."

34. Roger C. Vergin, "Computer-Induced Organizational Changes," in *The Impact of Information Technology on Management Operation*, ed. by William C. Hause (Princeton: Auerbach, 1971), pp. 180-81.

35. Ibid., pp. 183-86.

36. Thomas W. Weirich, "The Design of Information Systems," in *Leadership in Social Administration: Perspectives for the 1980s*, ed. by Felice Davidson Perlmutter & Simon Slavin (Philadelphia: Temple University Press, 1980), pp. 142-56.

37. George Hoshino, "Social Services: The Problem of Accountability," *Social Service Review*, 47 (September, 1973): 373-83; "The Age of Accountability," *Social Work*, 18 (January, 1973): 2, 114; Murray L. Gruber (ed.), *Management Systems in the Human Services* (Philadelphia: Temple University Press, 1981); E. Bartezzaghi et al., "Computers, Management and Organization: Reflections on a Pilot Study," *Information and Management*, 4 (November, 1981): 235-58; Philip Ein-Dor & Eli Segev, "Information Systems: Emergence of a New Organizational Function," *Information and Management*, 5 (September, November, 1982): 279-86; and Tony Moynihan, "Information Systems as Aids to Achieving Organizational Integration," *Information and Management*, 5 (September, November, 1982): 225-29.

38. David Easton, *A Systems Analysis of Political Life* (Chicago: University of Chicago Press, 1979), pp. 85-89 and 135-40.

39. Andrew M. Pettigrew, *The Politics of Organizational Decision Making* (London: Tavistock, 1973), pp. 229-30.

40. Schoech, *Computer Use in Human Services*, pp. 216-17.

41. Marion E. Weiner, *Human Services Management* (Homewood, IL: Dorsey Press, 1982), pp. 538-39.

42. For an overview of these and other related approaches, see Gruber, *Management in the Human Services* and Bageshwari Parihar, *Task-Centered Management in Human Services* (Springfield, IL: Charles C Thomas, 1984).

43. Stephen M. Druzner, "The Emerging Art of Decision-Making," *Social Casework*, 54 (January, 1973): 3-12; Chris Argyris & Donald A. Schon, *Theory in Practice: Increasing Professional Effectiveness* (San Francisco: Jossey-Bass, 1974).

44. Weirich, "The Design of Information Systems," pp. 148-50.

45. Ibid., pp. 148-49.

46. Ibid., p. 149.

47. Ibid., p. 150.

48. Ibid., p. 151.

49. Herbert Simon, *Administrative Behavior* (New York: The Free Press, 1965); and James D. Thompson, *Organizations in Action* (New York: McGraw-Hill, 1967).

50. Weirich, "The Design of Information Systems," p. 153.

Chapter 5

Technology, Information and Intentionality in the Human Services: The Larger Picture

INFORMATION, KNOWLEDGE AND LEGITIMACY

Any discussion of the extent to which computerized information systems eclipse human volition in human services requires an examination of the role of information and knowledge in contemporary society. It seems the reliance on rationally generated knowledge has so influenced the contemporary world view legitimate alternatives have been challenged. Legitimation invariably rests on normative structures. As organizational rationality spreads and develops to its current level of pervasiveness, it undermines and weakens cultural traditions nurturing normative structures of legitimacy. For example, as administrators and managers increasingly dominate the functions of government and the delivery of human services, purportedly to improve accountability and quality control, the traditions important for legitimation cannot be regenerated administratively and fall by the wayside.[1]

What replaced these traditions? This question occupied many important thinkers in the twentieth century: Max Horkeimer, Herbert Marcuse and Jurgen Habermas, all of the Frankfurt School of Social Research in Germany; Jacques Ellul and Jean-Francois Lyotard and others in France; and Daniel Boorstin, Paul Goodman, Daniel Bell and others in the United States. In many ways, these philosophers and social scientists addressed issues

Karl Marx raised in the nineteenth century. Marx argued the problems of technology were imbedded in a given social structure: technology is and must be used by its capitalist owners to dominate workers.[2]

Where Marx sought to demystify nineteenth-century capitalist economic ideology, the Frankfort School aimed at the illusions of twentieth-century capitalist and socialist ideologies. They argued that rationality itself is warped by domination and that domination may be inherent to political structures, such as those of the Soviet Union and, perhaps, more subtly, those of advanced capitalist states. Some of this domination is essentially related to science and technology.[3] Ellul viewed technology and efficiency as having replaced the values which might have nurtured other normative world views.[4] Lyotard examined "legitimation" in "post modern" society through the status of science, technology and the arts, the significance of technology, and the methods of control of the flow of information and knowledge in the Western world. Like Habermas, Lyotard asked: "How do we legitimate the criteria for sorting true statements from false?" While Lyotard focused his analysis in the realms of language and knowledge, Habermas extended his to questions of authority and consensus.[5]

In Daniel Bell's *The Coming of Post-Industrial Society* is serious and sustained investigation of post-industrial society, which he characterized as having experienced the "managerial revolution," he examined the growing importance of information and knowledge as productive forces, and the global proliferation of technology. Bell focused on the influence of technology, not as an autonomous factor[6] but ". . . as an analytical element, to see what social changes come in the wake of new technologies, and what problems the society, and its political system, must then attempt to solve." He viewed preindustrial society as one characterized as primarily "extractive," with an economy based on agriculture, mining, fishing, timber and other resources as natural gas or oil. In contrast, the industrial society is characterized as primarily "fabricating," using energy and machine technology for the manufacture of goods. The postindustrial society, in

Bell's definition is one of "processing" and telecommunications and computers are strategic to the exchange of information and knowledge.[7]

The huge explosion in news, statistical data and information makes it almost impossible to chart its expansion. The growth of scientific information, however, can be one index, the one Bell used to note its virtual geometric increase in amount. He described the creation of large-scale, national networks built by linking specialized centers and the automated data banks so basic scientific and technical data, whether from industrial plants or from medical institutions, can be retrieved directly from computers and transmitted to the user. The appearance of information services like DIALOG is an example. Proliferating scientific and other data bases, however, rest on the ability, increasingly more desirable, of constructing a program for use of a "knowledge base." Retrieving items from the census, which is a data base, is a relatively straightforward technical matter; but finding kindred and analogous concepts for the handling of ideas raises problems of a different intellectual order. Attempts to discipline human knowledge into a vast, unified edifice are invariably bound to fail, because using ideas in new, creative ways requires regrouping and recategorizing terms and concepts, and, in this creative process, no exhaustive set of permutations and combinations can do the task.[8] Nonetheless, the rather technically straightforward manner of programming data bases has superceded the conceptual construction of "knowledge bases."

An empirical examination of the extent to which programming data bases has eclipsed the conceptual construction of knowledge bases lays well beyond the scope of this book, as meritorious as such an undertaking would be. Hints can be gleaned, however, from discussions of the function and use of knowledge and information in contemporary society. Bell, for example, links the centrality of theoretical knowledge to an expansion of the service sector of the economy. In these economic processes, telecommunications and computers (hardware), accompanied by what he calls "intellectual technologies" or planning and decision-making, have become more crucial than property.[9] The very notion, however, of "intellectual technologies" suggests a saturated notion of technique in the contemporary world view. This technocratic world view emphasizes logical, practical, problem-solving, instrumental, orderly, and disciplined approaches to objectives. This view also relies on a calculus containing precision and measurement, and on a concept of a system. As such, the technocratic world view is quite opposed to the philosophical, historical, religious, esthetic and intuitive modes of inquiry.[10]

Boguslaw also addresses the question of the extent to which the importance of information and knowledge have come to dominate modern thought. In *The New Utopians*, he applies systems theory to business management and social planning. In the final chapter of this work, entitled "The Power of Systems and Systems of Power," Boguslaw discusses the implications of systems theory and its world view on bureaucracy and power. He uses Robert Bierstedt's definitions of power and authority,[11] in which power refers to the ability to apply force and authority refers to institutionalized power. For Bierstedt, in an idealized organization, power and authority become equivalent to each other. The right to use force is attached to certain levels of status within the organization. "You do this or receive an unsatisfactory rating" is characterized in the computer world a binary choice. The exercise of force is related to the range of alternatives made available. The person with the ability to specify alternatives is the one who possesses power.[12]

Systems designers and computer programmers possess power, according to Boguslaw, in the sense that, *de facto*, they have the prerogative to specify the range of phenomena a system will distinguish. This power is related directly to computer technology and the way it limits information and circumscribes knowledge. Boguslaw explains this as follows:

> The strength of high-speed computers lies precisely in their capacity to process binary choice data rapidly. But to process these data, the world of reality must at some point in time be reduced to binary form. This occurs initially through operational specifications handed to a computer

programmer. These specifications serve as a basis for more detailed reductions to binary choices. The range of possibilities is ultimately set by the circuitry of the computer, which places finite limits on alternatives for data storage and processing. The structure of the language used to communicate with the computer places additional restrictions on the range of alternatives. The programmer himself, through the specific sets of data he uses in his solution to a programming problem and the specific techniques he uses for his solution, places a final set of restrictions on action alternatives available within a computer-based system.[13]

To the extent decisions made in the design process by systems designers and computer programmers serve to reduce, limit or totally eliminate actions, designers are applying force and wielding power. Again, to the extent the use of computers and reliance on information systems pervade the administrative and clinical spheres of human service organizations, those who adhere to the technological world view invariably challenge those in the more traditional authority structure, who use processes based on tradition, precedent, practice wisdom, professional judgment, and experience.

INFORMATION SYSTEMS, VALUES AND INTENTIONALITY IN THE HUMAN SERVICES

Information systems exacerbate the all-too-common bureaucratic tendency to convert political and ethical issues to administrative or technical problems, to translate values into technical tasks.[14] Rationality rules. Although information-processing professionals seldom seem to have any discernible political ax to grind, values are basically prime factors, derived neither scientifically, logically nor intellectually. Values take into account preferences for desirable outcomes. Technology functions, as John McDermott claims, as an "opiate of the educated public today."[15] Technology carries with it high hopes for improvement, lulling into dormancy the critical and judgmental skills in society in general and in administrative and clinical practice in particular. Despite the practical importance of these techniques, institutions and processes of knowledge in contemporary society, administrative decision making and the resolution of personal and social problems by clinical professionals are clearly not dependent nor limited to knowledge and rationality by themselves.[16] People are not thinking machines nor can human expertise be reduced to mechanical principles.[17]

Science-based decision-making techniques have their appeal because they call for clarity: in the specification of goals, we are offered the illusion, particularly in the human services, that value preferences are clear. The effectiveness of systems analysis depends on having explicitly stated objectives and evaluation criteria at the start; these criteria and specific action objectives invariably relate to society's system of values. The application of systems analysis to the human services tends to downplay the value conflicts inherent to organizational decision making and clinical practice and stress a process of decision making and problem resolution which differs significantly from administrators' and clinicians' experience.

The extent to which "technocrats" and their ethos have come to displace human intentionality or will in the planning and administration as well as in the direct delivery of human services is a major concern. Hoshino and others have noted the notion of accountability dominated social services delivery for 10 to 15 years. The 1960s analysis of social welfare programs gave way to a decade or so of monitoring and evaluating programs on the basis of their effectiveness, called accountability. Users and funders cried: "Prove it. Prove resources are allocated wisely, people benefit, the best possible, most needed services are provided with the money and talent available." "Better management" was the reply, with its host of techniques such as management by objectives (MBO) and program planning and budgeting systems (PPBS).[18]

There were those, however, who, rather critically, looked at a phenomenon they perceived as a "revolution of unknown proportions." Gruber, for example, noted spiraling expenditures and spreading bureaucratization generated a call for efficiency both liberals and conservatives could espouse. This push shifted the human services, as exemplified by the state welfare programs, from such concerns as social equity and democratic planning to the technocratic notions of "product," "output" and "efficiency." Technological optimists viewed systems sciences, management sciences and the information explosion as new arenas for social management and control, a kind of technological utopia blotting out the last vestiges of man's irrationality and capriciousness. Pessimists, however, saw these developments as a monstrous system of "total administration" canceling man, robbing him of intentionality and will and eclipsing values, not through terror, brutality and authoritarianism, but "through gradual subjugation in the reasonable name of efficient problem solving."[19]

Gruber charts the extent to which the technological notion of efficiency has been woven into social structures and the human services. Rationality is at the heart of the systems perspective. Applications of systems sciences, especially the engineering control processes found in systems management, systems engineering, operations research and input-output analysis, are intensified by an economizing spirit. This urge to "get the most from the least" results in rationalizing the budgetary process, allocating resources efficiently and monitoring and evaluating social programs. These control processes pervade welfare, education, health, urban planning, corrections, law enforcement and other fields involving social management. The Rand Corporation, for example, which has pioneered development of analytic techniques and management skills advises New York City on major social administration questions. The Bendix International Aerospace Systems Division established an Urban/Environmental Systems Group to consult in social agency planning, program evaluation, data systems analysis, socioeconomic cost-benefit studies, and information requirements in criminal justice, population planning and drug abuse. Corporate enterprise, with its "big business," efficiency-oriented mindset, is best represented by the membership of boards of directors such as those of the local United Way.[20]

Management has witnessed the influx and influence of systems and engineering theory, decision theory, cybernetics, information processing, game theory, linear programming, queuing theory, PERT charts, and scheduling and network analysis. Devised for application to central problems of strategic choice, these concepts and techniques are instruments for managing complex situations so limited resources can be deployed for maximum benefits. The ideology of efficiency owes a large debt to Taylor's scientific management. Taylor's concept, there is "one best way" of doing a job, spread from the early 20th-century factory and material industries to knowledge, the "education industry" and also to home, family and church.[21] Robert McNamara created a new office, deputy assistant for systems analysis, to introduce the planning-programming-budgeting system (PPBS), a system developed by the Rand Corporation for assessing costs and choices in relation to Department of Defense strategy. His 1960-65 "revolution" was an attempt to rationalize a government structure, using a full array of systems management techniques.[22]

This world view, based on systems management techniques, has extended its hegemony to education, health planning, social services and urban planning. It has brought with it — and made a virtue of — impersonal measurement. People simply recede from view, lost in the abstract labyrinths of systems models and input-output black boxes. At best, people are cogs in the machine, inputs or resources to be managed to produce outcome in the desired amount and of maximum quality. In human services, John Rubell, a former assistant secretary of defense and a senior vice president of Litton Industries, helped plan the War on Poverty. He proposed the Job Corps training centers be designed by large corporations that had designed and managed some of the more complex weapons systems for the Defense Department. He viewed the Job Corps as a complex machine transforming people. Rubell made vivid the view of the Job Corps in particular and human service organizations in general as "people-processing organizations."[23]

The people-processing organization, just as have industry and business, has succumbed to the lure of systems management and efficiency experts. In public welfare, for instance, there is a striking example. The American Public Welfare Association (APWA), providing consultation to states, offers the "one best way" to organize a benefits system. Its model proposes a type of organization which depends on hierarchical authority and detailed specifications for machine-tooling behavior. APWA explains:

> A smooth working organization . . . requires precise specification of authority and responsibility with a single source of authority and defined responsibility for each position in the agency. Otherwise, disorganization, confusion and irresponsibility result. . . . Job descriptions must carry the appropriate and precise descriptions for each position.[24]

This new rationality in public welfare specifies in minute detail what is to be done, how it is to be done, by whom and the time allowed. Standard input-output analysis is applied to the entire workflow and client movement through the system. APWA and other technical manuals paint a picture of carefully planned, allocated management — complete with workflow diagrams, elaborate job descriptions, organization charts, span of control (the specification of the number of supervisees per supervisor), prescriptions, the scalar principle (non-overlapping and vertical authority system), plus computerized management information systems to monitor clients and workers — a stunning illusion of a rationally designed organization.[25]

The rational approach to human service delivery requires the development of and adherence to blueprints and models expunging human agency, will and intentionality. Although blueprints and plans cannot compel people to obey, men can be made obedient. Since these systems cancel the human factor, the concept of the person as a responsible agent of decision vanishes and capitulation to the blueprint follows. As technique progressively pervades the human service arena, the administration of systems

becomes the administration of things — of targets, target popula-
tions, inputs, outputs, raw materials, products — and people become objects or components because human agency and intentionality have ceased.[26]

On the heels of such models of rational administration as
PPBS and MBO came the promises of management information
systems (MIS). Funding bodies are requiring massive amounts of
information about services from most agencies and, more and
more often, agencies are struggling to implement computer-
based information systems. By and large, however, MIS like
PPBS and MBO, mimics a technological view which tends to
exclude larger human, organizational and social considerations.
It skirts the reality that too many agencies have structural problems and poor communication systems. Instead, it replicates and
amplifies these weaknesses and is, therefore, system-conserving
in the worst sense. Emphasizing the technical optimum of the
MIS beclouds organizational questions such as the extent of integration or centralization of services desired. Achieving technical
optimality may very well increase these problems and, in the
end, override considerations for change deference to the technical optimality itself. Thus, technical optimality becomes the
guiding principle or main criterion for decisions and takes precedence over more political, if not intentional or willful, aspects of
decision making.[27]

Couched in terms of functions, the MIS speaks the language of
system maintenance, masking conflict. The language of systems
and functions seems clear and harmonious, in which power is a
word seldom used. If one steps away from technological language and into political language, an entirely new, not so clear
and not so harmonious reality is created: the hurly-burly of decisions, of competing purposes, conflicts and interests. Decisions
about program options, preferences, service priorities and service mixes — in short, who to serve and how — are fraught with
interest and controversy, as are the various other decisions of
resource allocation plaguing policy makers and agency executives.[28]

On the whole, implementing MIS brings commitment to the

technological viewpoint, to the world view endemic to technique. Technical optimality and efficiency not only mask purposes, eclipse human intentionality in decision making, they present an alternative, a formidable counterpoint, to formal authority ordinarily residing in position and expertise. To the extent human services administrators adhere to more traditional roles such as mediating between conflicting interests, creating an environment in which others do their jobs, coordinating activities and resources, they retain political and ethical roles at variance with the technological one. If, however, administrators buy into the technological viewpoint and many have, they run the risk of creating and legitimating an authority structure eclipsing the authority of those steeped in precedence, traditions, professional judgments and practice wisdom.

TECHNOLITICS: TECHNOLOGY AND POLITICS IN THE HUMAN SERVICES: A BALANCED AFFIRMATION

The term "technolitics" might convey the idea that technology supercedes politics, but it can also mean technology and power (and authority) are coequal, symbiotic components of decision making in the human services. I coined "technolitics" rather irrationally, for its crisp ring, just like the phrase "clockwork orange." Despite the pervasiveness of technique and rationality, the all too human aesthetic appreciation lead to the choice of technolitics. It reflects an affirmation of both rational and political decision making, despite the seemingly mechanical nature of the former and the apparently arbitrary nature of the latter.

The concepts of technology and bureaucracy are linked by a rational approach to problem solving and getting things done, usually in the name of efficiency. At their most extremely negative, both technology and bureaucracy threaten those aspects of man's existence held most dearly: intentionality, will, agency and democracy. Paradoxically, the rise of bureaucracy and the appeal of technology was an apparent ability to circumvent capriciousness, arbitrariness, whim, and other less desirable aspects of human behavior. Taken to extreme, however, technology and bureaucracy are also less than desirable. One way out of the morass bureaucratic and technologic extremes is a middle ground, extracting the positive aspects of each while submitting both to critical scrutiny. This exercise, in and of itself, shows faith in our ability to direct what appear to be determining factors in our lives. An attempt to reconcile the opprobrious results of unfettered technology and bureaucracy reveals hidden faith in our ability to do so, to bring about a more desirable set of circumstances or to place extremes in a more balanced perspective.[29]

Reconciling the adverse consequences of technology and bureaucracy enhances the political and ethical aspects of human behavior and reasserts the primacy of participation in decision-making processes. Technology and bureaucracy in extreme make man apolitical and nonethical. This reaches its highest level of paradox in the human services, services intended to enhance the dignity and self-determination of clients. Dignity and self-determination lay in people's abilities to participate in decisions and actions affecting their lives and taking responsibility for the consequences of those decisions and actions. To the extent information systems and that world view dominate human services, there may be highly paradoxical and, perhaps, negative consequences.

Some intellectual housecleaning will bury the technically self-serving myth that technology and bureaucracy are neutral until humans endow them with purpose. Both technology and bureaucracy describe actions. Not only can action not be neutral, but the potential for technology and bureaucracy are circumscribed by that technology and bureaucracy. Furthermore, computer-based information systems reinforce a world view, a way of thinking and perceiving, decisively apolitical. Information systems tend to conceal purpose, values, intentionality, interest and controversy. The criteria for technical and bureaucratic systems are self-referential; they tend to be technical or rational, not social nor political. Technicism and bureaucratization, of which information systems and scientific management are examples as well as indices, imply a world view, a mental environment, in which the vocabulary of agents and intentions has been displaced by one of surface composure and order, routine and predictability. This is the world of bureaucratic-managerial and technical elites, a world that transforms problems of political interest into purely technical problems. The current structure of the MIS encourages people to displace their freedom to decide onto experts of all sorts, particularly on information and computer experts, and, in doing so, lose human power and dignity.[30]

These dangers are not inevitable. In the years ahead, power increasingly will be based on access to or control of information, a substantial political component to management and information systems. Making this component clear and obvious means the groundwork can be laid for an open process, one involving collaboration between administrators, information systems experts, and clinicians within human service agencies and, outside, with planners, politicians, and the public. This is a call for a genuinely participative technology.[31]

The manner and extent of participation are difficult questions only to be mentioned in the present context. Abrahamsson, for example, suggests two kinds of participation, one extending the role of employees in management and the other increasing worker involvement in the implementation of decisions made at higher levels.[32] Both are necessary to offset the threat to basic democratic participatory principles. It is widely acknowledged that technology and bureaucracy pose a threat to basic democratic, participatory principles, but they do serve as bulwarks against partisan groups, be they clinicians, administrators, or even technicians. Etzioni-Halevy, for example, notes the paradoxical nature of bureaucratic development: it is both a threat to and a requirement of democracy. In practically all Western countries, bureaucracies are both subject to political control when devising and implementing public sector policy and free from such control with respect to partisan interest.[33] Although many human service agencies are in the private sector, their bureaucratic apparatus is controlled by boards of directors who determine the agency's mission, one laced with rules and regulations which minimize partisan interests. Thus, it can be argued bureaucracy is a social invention to promote such humanly desirable ends as fairness and merit which also gets things done with some degree of efficiency, productivity and innovation, and is a means of providing a structure for creativity.[34]

Technology has had its apostles, announcing the potential for democratization brought by the proliferation of personal computers. Toffler, for example, pronounced the end of organization man and technocracy, and of "the modular man" and the coming of organizational "ad-hocracy." Toffler's Third Wave, highly technical, civilization shattered the fortress of managerial power, "that pyramidical bastion of managerial experts and super elites who seized the "means of integration," technology, and the "reins of social, cultural, political, and economic control," characteristic of Second Wave, industrial society.[35]

In Third Wave society, "the control of information, privacy, and the management of information flow" become increasingly important. Meta-information becomes the key to control; power no longer equals knowledge, but rather "knowledge about knowledge." In this argument, the diversity and availability of communication devices and channels will make Third Wave society more democratic than Second Wave industrial society. Tape recorders, paper copiers, even cable television, are all communications tools aimed at the general consumer, whose use is difficult to control. Toffler claims computer use makes the "demassifying" of society technically feasible; there will be an increase in participation in decision-making processes affecting society in general and organizations in particular.[36]

Another apostle of technology, John Naisbett provided a roadmap to the twenty first century. He identified ten mega-trends, most pronounced of which were shifts from an industrial to an information society, from centralized political, organizational and administrative structures to decentralized ones, and from pyramidical hierarchies to participatory networks. Naisbett dated the advent of information society to 1956 and 1957, when white collar workers or those in technical, managerial and clerical positions began to outnumber blue collar workers, and the Russians, by launching Sputnik, inaugurated the era of global satellite communications. In his "Information Society," information replaces capital as strategic resource, in the hands of many, it displaces money as the source of power and a knowledge theory of value eclipses a labor theory of value.[37]

Far from fostering technical determinism inimical to man's development, technology and information systems, assert the Tofflers and Naisbetts of the world, promote open-ended systems that maximize participation and choice. Perhaps the most unequivocally optimistic outlook comes from Jeremy Campbell, the Washington correspondent for the London Standard. The "lesson of information theory," Campbell writes, is basically a balance between choice and constraint, which lead not toward oneness or sameness, the way of entropy, but rather toward the "genuinely new" and the "endlessly complex" products of mind and nature, the way of history.[38]

The optimistic forays into the nature of man and the impact on it of technology and bureaucracy are a striking contrast to more pessimistic views. Barrett, for example, traces the elimination of such concepts as self and soul from the vocabulary and scrutiny of philosophical discourse, thereby resulting in a depreciation of human life.[39] Montagu and Matson describes "technological dehumanization," or the reduction of man to machines, the exegetic scrutiny of "postmodern society" by Marx, Freud, Durkheim, Weber and Simmel. Such apprehension has been a recurrent theme of fantasy and science fiction since Mary Shelly's 1818 vision of the first "cyborg" (cybernetic organism). Some have seen this mechanical pathology as a new type of social character not so much deviant as mutant — an organic combination of man and machine. Lewis Yablonsky names this freak product of cultural evolution the "robopath." The creatures of a culture which worships mechanical efficiency, regularity and predictability, robopaths are individuals "whose pathology entails robot-like behavior and existence . . . they are people who simulate machines."[40] The robopathic personality is rigidly conformist, compulsively orderly and efficient, unemotional and unspontaneous, and unquestionably obedient to authority.[41]

At the other extreme is the cheerful robot, another byproduct of technological society. S/he is characterized less by alienation and discontent than by adaptation and contentment, not the disaffiliated stranger but the Organization Man. When social scientists were becoming concerned with the spread of technical organization and mechanical routine, C. Wright Mills was especially fearful for the survival of freedom and reason and the autonomous individual in the mass society and mass culture. He saw an emerging socially adjusted and willingly compliant individual for whom both routine and the distraction from routine were not only acceptable, but "meaningful" — and to whom therefore the burdensome issues of personal freedom and independent thought have become irrelevant and even suspect. These people alarmed him. "It will no longer do," Mills wrote, "merely to assume, as a metaphysic of human nature, that down deep in man-as-man there is an urge for freedom and a will to reason."[42] Too many people seemed prepared to shrug off their own freedom, to go willingly into the mindlessness of compulsive conformity, ritualized behavior, and automated existence.[43]

These images of man, whether of the pathologically pessimistic variety or of mundane mindlessness, underscore the need to affirm our responsibility as individuals to transcend technological and all other determinants of human action. Many have explored the roles of intentionality and will in the development of personality and society. After such nineteenth century philosophers and social scientists as Hegel, Darwin, Marx and Spencer, each of whom perceived life as the captive of a system of mechanics with workings beyond an individual's reach to either influence profoundly or to alter, came the likes of Lester Ward, William James and John Dewey. These philosophers and social scientists subscribed to a doctrine of progress contingent upon the contributions which people are willing to risk toward its realization. Their pragmatic philosophy held that man's fate was not determined by mechanical powers, but by man himself, and insisted man could create as well as succumb to the environment.[44] More contemporary figures, including Paul Ricoeur and Martin Heidegger, articulate a concept of volition for technological advances, and include Robert Heilbroner who analyzes the application of technology through social influences.[45]

Human intentionality and will in the technological age encompass values, ethics and responsibility in society in general and in human service organizations in particular. Arguments about the direction of influence between technology and values have yielded consensus they are independent. Although some philosophers, Alan Gewirth, for example, have painstakingly constructed ethical frameworks on rationality, the is-ought question continues to be heavily debated, since values determine ethical principles.[46] Mesthene, for example, is a firm advocate of what Weinberg calls the "technological fix," in which many social and technical problems can best be dealt with by further advances. Admittedly, full implementation of technological opportunities may require transformations in social values. But even when such changes undermine traditional values, the need for the act of determining value itself remains. In a way, technology makes the intelligent exercise of values more critical. Technique and the technological viewpoint have inundated and pervaded contemporary life in general and the organization and delivery of human services in particular making the act of determining value all that much more valuable.[47]

Ethical-political issues in technology received progressively more recognition from the 1960s until recently on the problems of pollution and environmental deterioration. The disciplines of technological assessment (TA) and environmental ethics emerged from this focus. TA was a narrow, problem-oriented discipline, originally conceived to investigate second-order consequences of specific technological projects, in order to facilitate the decision-making process. In doing so, TA dealt with questions of value. Environmental ethicists seek to extend man's responsibilities to the natural world, an extension which has received its most complete expression in Hans Jonas' works on the ethics of technology, part of his influential work on religious thought, the philosophy of biology, and the historico-philosophical origins of modern technology.[48]

Manfred Stanley, however, places moral responsibility squarely on the shoulders of policy formers in a world dominated by technological viewpoints he calls technicism and pantechnicism. In the latter term, he meant to capture the way technicism came to dominate even metaphorical and symbolic language, not just concrete problem solving.[49] For Stanley, people cannot escape their moral agency, not even by delegating it to experts. It is in the realm of public policy that moral agency finds its most tangible expression. Generally, policy is organized conduct oriented toward commonly valued ends. It is morally informed and intentional conduct, not simply technologically rational behavior related to precisely specified goals. Policies, in short, are not merely techniques. Morally informed, policies are inherently political, in that competing values vie to dominate the determination of commonly valued ends, which may change over time.[50]

At the heart of reconciling technology and policy, of emancipating man from believing technology must rule life, supercede all other forms of authority, tradition and thought, lay technolitics, a commitment to affirm both technology and politics and the kind of systems view that will predominate. Will the new systems view broaden participation and make competing values in the development of services explicit or will it lead to a mythically value-neutral "rationalization" of services based on top-down control? The choice is technocracy or participation.[51]

Paradoxically, technological changes in society have produced an increased number of professional and scientific workers whose education and training conditions them to preserve autonomy by deciding what work to do, how to do it and even when to do it.[52] Because there is a high degree of professionalism in human service organizations, they stand at the crossroads of an increasingly technocratic mode of acting and thinking, or they can open the design and development of information systems to all interested parties. Despite paeans to the contrary, powerful forces are pushing human service administrators in the technocratic direction.[53]

Funding agencies, for example, often insist on quick, measurable results to which administrators all too frequently respond with narrow measures such as case-load summaries and work-load distribution. Broad measures such as community impact and involvement will be ignored, because they are much softer in character, even though the level of community participation that went into their development makes them legitimate. These are not measures of "objective" conditions, or of the one best way to achieve a desired outcome, but rather, reflect the degree, quality and nature of consensus on the impact of the service among all interested participants.[54]

In the human services, overemphasis on accountability and the use of such rational means as information systems and computers have the effect of placing the technical above the moral, political, and social components of people's lives. Recent trends toward accountability and computer-generated information systems may cause human service organizations entire working operations to be symbolically, as well as actually, reconstituted into one interlocking problem-solving system, acting under technological control. Other forms of control still compete with the technological: bureaucracy's inherent formal authority also a rational calculus for getting things done efficiently. However, combination of technology and bureaucracy produces a sense of mindlessness, which undermining traditional social meanings and affects bureaucratic forms of authority and control.[55]

Exiting from this morass lays in development and implementation of more participative forms of control focusing on the discussion of values and ends. Debating the technical and the political aspects of the desirability and value of ends and means is of paramount importance. Values and ethics are interwoven with the responsibilities of human services administrators and clinicians.[56] Administrators, professionals, planners and evaluators all can determine the character and potential of tomorrow's human service agency. Accountability at all levels, service, funding and planning, is fundamental to sustain the democratic power of contemporary society. But, essential also is broad participatory planning in which process, context and system are the key organizing terms.[57]

As the organizing principle, technolitics fuses the technological and political processes through public discussion in society and participative management at the organizational level. To the extent information systems can inform participants and decision makers on matters of service goals and policy formation, so much the better. To the extent the fusion of technology and politics, technolitics, with its required participatory decision making, becomes a way of thinking about human services and society, then the further we will move, as Boulding notes, toward "human betterment."[58]

SUMMARY

A world view of technical rationality currently pervades contemporary thought to the extent that, for many, it replaces alternative values which, in turn, might have nurtured other norms. In this technocratic world view, what is rational and technical seems right, emphasizing the logical and instrumental approach to meeting objectives. It relies on a calculus of precision and measurement and a homeostatically functioning system. The technocratic world view is quite opposed to philosophical, historical, religious, esthetic and intuitive modes of inquiry which also seek to provide understanding and guide human actions. The use of computers and the reliance on information systems indicate the pervasiveness of the technological world view.

Under the guise of accountability, this technological world view has come to dominate the human services. Throughout the 1970s and 1980s, a myriad of management strategies, such as MBO and PPBS, were applied in human service settings. Efficiency became the desideratum; monitoring the process, the means. Management witnessed the influx and influence of systems and engineering theories, decision theory, cybernetics, information processing, game theory, linear programming, queuing theory, PERT charts, network analysis, time-series studies and other. Impersonal measurement became a virtue in honor of the god accountability.

Within this technical-managerial world view, people virtually disappear, lost in abstract labyrinths of systems models and input-output black boxes. At best, people are cogs in the machine, seen as inputs or resources to be managed so that outcomes will be in the desired amount and of the maximum quality. Expunged are human agency, will and intentionality. The system and its blueprint dominate.

By and large, MIS both exemplifies and harbors a technological viewpoint which excludes larger human, organizational and social considerations. Emphasis on achieving the technical optimum of the MIS beclouds such organizational questions as the desired extent of integration or centralization of services. It glosses over conflicts inherent in the hurly-burly of decision making. Decisions about program options, preferences, service priorities and service mixes are fraught with interests and controversies. So, too are the various other decisions about resource allocation plaguing policy makers and agency executives.

Technology and bureaucracy are integral aspects of modern society. Both have positive and negative consequences on the quality of human life. Neither is inherently totalitarian nor liberating. Neither is value free. Each contains aspects of dominance as well as liberation. The neologism "technolitics" reflects affirmation of both rational and political decision making, stating a middle ground on which to extract the positive aspects of each and submit them to critical scrutiny with open, public participation.

The challenge ahead is to clarify the political component of the technological and bureaucratic processes dominating the administration of human services. The exit from the morass of excessive attention to rational accountability schemes indicated by MIS usage lays in the developing and implementing more participative forms of control, ones that focus publicly on discussing values and ends. Administrators, professionals, planners and evaluators all can determine the character and potential of today's human service agency in tomorrow's world.

NOTES

1. Jurgen Habermas, *Legitimation Crisis* (Boston: Beacon Press, 1975), p. 47.

2. Carl Mitchum, "Philosophy of Technology," in Paul T. Dubin (ed.), *A Guide to the Culture of Science, Technology, and Medicine* (New York: The Free Press, 1984), p. 235.

3. Ibid., p. 336.

4. See for example, Jacques Ellul, *The Technological System* (New York: Continuum, 1980); and *The Technological Society* (New York: Vintage Books, 1964).

5. Habermas, *Legitimation Crisis*; Jean-Francois Lyotard, *The Postmodern Condition: A Report on Knowledge* (Minneapolis: University of Minnesota Press, 1984).

6. See Langdon Winner, *Autonomous Technology: Techniques-Out-of-Control as a Theme in Political Thought* (Cambridge, MA: MIT Press, 1977).

7. Daniel Bell, *The Coming of Post-Industrial Society: A Venture in Social Forecasting* (New York: Basic Books, 1973), p. xii.

8. Daniel Bell, "Teletext and Technology: New Networks of Knowledge and Information in Postindustrial Society," in *The Winding Passage: Essays and Sociological Journeys, 1960-1980* (New York: Basic Books, 1980), pp. 34-65.

9. Mitchum, "Philosophy of Technology," p. 336; Bell, *The Coming of Post-Industrial Society*; and Bell, "The Social Framework of the Information Society," in Tom Forester (ed.), *The Microelectronics Revolution* (Cambridge, MA: MIT Press, 1980), pp. 500-49.

10. Bell, *The Coming of Post-Industrial Society*, pp. 348-51.

11. Robert Bierstedt, "An Analysis of Social Power," *American Sociological Review*, 15 (December, 1950): 730-38.

12. Robert Boguslaw, *The New Utopians: A Study of System Design and Social Change* (Enlarged ed.; New York: Irvington, 1981), pp. 187-90.

13. Ibid., p. 190.

14. Herbert Marcuse, *One Dimensional Man* (Boston: Beacon Press, 1964), p. 232.

15. John McDermit, "Technology: The Opiate of the Intellectuals," in Albert H. Teich (ed.), *Technology and Man's Future* (2nd ed.; New York: St. Martin's Press, 1977), pp. 180-207.

16. Emmanuel G. Methene, "The Role of Technology in Society," in Teich, op. cit., pp. 165-180.

17. Sherry Turkle, *The Second Self: Computers and the Human Spirit* (New York: Simon and Schuster, 1985); and Hurbert L. Dreyfus & Stuart E. Dreyfus, *Mind Over Machine: The Power of Human Intuition and Expertise in the Era of the Computer* (New York: The Free Press, 1986).

18. George Hoshino, "Social Services: The Problem of Accountability," *Social Service Review*, 47 (September, 1973): 373-83; Jerry S. Turem, "The Call for a Management Stance," *Social Work*, 19 (September, 1974): 615-23; Murray Gruber (ed.), *Management Systems in the Human Services* (Philadelphia: Temple University Press, 1981).

19. Murray Gruber, "Total Administration," *Social Work*, 19 (September, 1974): 625.

20. Ibid., pp. 625-26.

21. See, for example, Frederick W. Taylor, *Scientific Management* (New York: Harper & Bros., 1911) and R. E. Callahan, *Education and the Cult of Efficiency* (Chicago: University of Chicago Press, 1962).

22. Gruber, "Total Administration," p. 628.

23. Ibid., p. 629.

24. Quote appears in ibid., p. 630.

25. Ibid.; for examples, see Jack C. Bloedorn et al., *Designing Social Service Systems* (Chicago: American Public Welfare Association, 1970); *Detailed Design of a Social Service Delivery System for the Bureau of Social Welfare, Department of Health and Welfare, State of Maine* (Chicago: Technical Assistance Project, American Public Welfare Association, July, 1970); Project Share, *Planning and Implementing Social Service Information Systems: A Guide for Management and Users* (Human Services Monograph No. 25, September, 1981, Aspen Systems Corp.).

26. Gruber, "Total Administration," p. 634.

27. Murray L. Gruber, Richard K. Caputo & Thomas Meenaghan, "Information Management," in Felice Davidson Perlmutter (ed.), *Human Services at Risk: Administrative Strategies for Survival* (Lexington, MA: Lexington Books, 1984), pp. 134-55.

28. Ibid., p. 136; Jean Hardy, *Values in Social Policy: Nine Contradictions* (London: Routledge & Kegan Paul, 1981), pp. 65-75.

29. For discussions of the adverse consequences of bureaucracy and technology, see, in addition to the several works already cited, David Burnham, *The Rise of the Computer State* (New York: Vintage Books, 1983); Henry Jacoby, *The Bureaucratization of the World* (Berkeley: University of California Press); Eva Etzioni-Halevy, *Bureaucracy and Democracy: A Political Dilemma* (London: Routledge & Kegan Paul, 1983); and Douglas Yates, *Bureaucratic Democracy: The Search for Democracy in American Government* (Cambridge, MA: Harvard University Press, 1982).

30. Gruber, Caputo & Meenaghan, "Information Management," pp. 144-45.

31. Ibid., p. 145; James D. Carrol, "Participatory Technology," *Science*, 171 (February, 1971): 647-53; Theodore Lowi, "The Political Impact of Information," in Forester (ed.), *The Microelectronics Revolution*, pp. 453-72.

32. Bengt Abrahamsson, *Bureaucracy or Participation: The Logic of Organization*. Beverly Hills, CA: Sage, 1977, pp. 189-91.

33. Etzioni-Halevy, *Bureaucracy and Democracy*, pp. 226-28; and Yates, *Bureaucratic Democracy*, pp. 177-205.

34. Charles T. Goodsell, *The Case For Bureaucracy: A Public Administration Polemic* (Chatham, NJ: Chatham House, 1983), pp. 139-46.

35. Alvin Toffler, *Future Shock* (New York: Bantam Books, 1970) and *The Third Wave* (New York: Bantam Books, 1980).

36. Alvin Toffler, *Previews and Premises* (New York: William Morrow, 1983).

37. John Naisbett, *Megatrends* (New York: Warner Books, 1984). See also Naisbett & Patricia Aburdene, *Reinventing the Corporation: Transforming Your Job and Your Company for the New Information Society* (New York: Warner Books, 1985).

38. Jeremy Campbell, *Grammatical Man: Information, Entropy, Language, and Life* (New York: Simon and Schuster, 1982).

39. William Barrett, *Death of the Soul: From Descartes to the Computer* (Garden City, NY: Anchor Press/Doubleday, 1986).

40. Lewis Yablonsky, *Robopaths* (Indianapolis: Bobbs-Merrill, 1972), p. 7. Quote also appears in Ashley Montagu & Floyd Matson, *The Dehumanization of Man* (New York: McGraw-Hill, 1983), p. 10.

41. Montagu & Matson, op. cit., pp. 9-12.

42. C. Wright Mills, *The Sociological Imagination* (New York: Oxford University Press, 1959). Quote appears in Montagu & Matson, op. cit., p. 25. For a classic expression of contemporary man's flight from freedom, see Eric Fromm, *Escape From Freedom* (New York: Avon Books, 1969).

43. Montagu & Matson, op. cit., pp. 24-26.

44. For a summary of this thought, see Richard K. Caputo, "Welfare And Freedom American Style" (Ph.D. dissertation, University of Chicago, 1982), pp. 22-25.

45. For a summary of the existential views of Ricoeur and Heidegger, see Mitchum, "Philosophy of Technology," pp. 317-22. For a more socio-political point of view, see Robert L. Heilbroner, *An Inquiry into the Human Prospect* (New York: W. W. Norton, 1974) and his chapter "Technological Determinism" in *Between Capitalism and Socialism: Essays in Political Economics* (New York: Vintage Books, 1970), pp. 147-64.

46. Alan Gewirth, *Reason and Morality* (Chicago: University of Chicago Press, 1978); and William K. Frankena, *Ethics* (2nd ed.; Englewood Cliffs, NJ: Prentice-Hall, 1973).

47. Mitchum, "Philosophy of Technology," p. 330; Emmanuel G. Mesthene, *Technological Change: Its Impact on Man and Society* (Cambridge, MA: Harvard University Press; New York: New American Library, 1970); Alvin M. Weinberg, "Can Technology Replace Social Engineering?" *Bulletin of the Atomic Scientists*, 22 (December, 1966): 4-8 [reprinted in Teich (ed.), *Technology and Man's Future*, pp. 22-30]; and Albert Borgmann, *Technology and the Character of Contemporary Life: A Philosophical Inquiry* (Chicago: University of Chicago Press, 1984).

48. Hans Jonas, "Technology and Responsibility: Reflections on the New Tasks of Ethics," *Social Research*, 15 (Spring, 1973): 160-80; "Responsibility Today: The Ethics of an Endangered Future," *Social Research*, 43 (Spring, 1976): 77-97; and *The Imperative of Responsibility: In Search of an Ethics for the Technological Age* (Chicago: University of Chicago Press, 1984). For a summary of Jones's philosophy, see Mitchum, "Philosophy of Technology," pp. 331-33.

49. Manfred Stanley, *The Technological Conscience: Survival and Dignity in an Age of Expertise* (Phoenix Edition; Chicago: University of Chicago Press, 1978), pp. 123-24.

50. Ibid., p. 232.

51. Larry Hirschhorn, "Evaluation and Administration: From Experimental Design to Social Planning," in Felice Davidson Perlmutter & Simon Slavin (eds.), *Leadership in Social Administration: Perspectives for the 1980s* (Philadelphia: Temple University Press, 1980), p. 189.

52. Eli Ginzberg, "The Mechanization of Work," *Scientific American*, 247 (September, 1982): 67-75.

53. Langdon Winner, *The Whale and the Reactor: A Search for Limits in an Age of High Technology* (Chicago: University of Chicago Press, 1986); and Theodore Roszak, *The Cult of Information: The Folklore of Computers and the True Art of Thinking* (New York: Pantheon Books, 1986).

54. Hirschhorn, "Evaluation and Administration," pp. 189-90.

55. For a description of this homeless aspect of modern consciousness, see Peter Berger et al., *The Homeless Mind: Modernization and Consciousness* (New York: Vintage Books, 1973).

56. Charles S. Levy, *Guide to Ethical Decisions and Actions for Social Service Administrators: A Handbook for Managerial Personnel* (New York: Haworth Press, 1982) and "Code of Ethics of the National Association of Social Workers" (Washington, DC: National Association of Social Workers, Inc., 1979).

57. Hirschhorn, "Evaluation and Administration," p. 191.

58. Kenneth Boulding, *Human Betterment* (Beverly Hills: Sage, 1985), particularly pp. 9-29 and 55-92.

Bibliography

BOOKS

Abrams, Gene M. "Supervision as Metatherapy." *Supervision, Consultation, and Staff Training in the Helping Professions*, ed. by Florence Whiteman Kaslow and Associates. San Francisco: Jossey-Bass, 1977.

Ahituv, Niu & Seev Neumann. *Principles of Information Systems for Management*. Dubuque, IA: Wm. C. Brown, 1982.

Argyris, Chris & Donald A. Schon. *Theory in Practice: Increasing Professional Effectiveness*. San Francisco: Jossey-Bass, 1974.

Argyris, Chris. *The Applicability of Organizational Sociology*. Cambridge: Cambridge University Press, 1972.

Argyris, Chris. *Organization and Innovation*. Homewood, IL: Richard D. Irwin and Dorsey Press, 1965.

Argyris, Chris. *Understanding Organizational Behavior*. Homewood, IL: Dorsey Press, 1960.

Bacharach, Samuel B. & Edward J. Lawler. *Power and Politics in Organizations*. San Francisco: Jossey-Bass, 1980.

Bakke, E. Wight. *Organizational Structure and Dynamics: A Framework for Theory*. New Haven: Labor and Management Center, Yale University, 1954.

Barrett, William. *Death of the Soul: From Descartes to the Computer*. Garden City, NJ: Anchor Press/Doubleday, 1986.

Barrett, William. *The Illusion of Technique: A Search for Meaning in a Technological Civilization*. Garden City, NY: Anchor Press/Doubleday, 1978.

Bell, Daniel. *The End of Ideology*. New York: The Free Press, 1960.

Bell, Daniel. "The Social Framework of the Information Society." In Tom Forester (ed.), *The Microelectronics Revolution: The Complete Guide to the New Technology and its Impact on Society*. Cambridge, MA: MIT Press, 1980.

Bell, Daniel. "Teletext and Technology: New Networks of Knowledge and Information in Postindustrial Society." *The Winding Passage: Essays and Sociological Journeys, 1960-1980*. New York: Basic Books, 1980.

Berger, Peter, Brigitte Berger & Hansfried Kellner. *The Homeless Mind: Modernization and Consciousness*. New York: Vintage Books, 1973.

Bernstein, Richard J. *The Restructuring of Social and Political Theory*. New York: Harcourt Brace Jovanovich, 1976.

Black, James Menzies. *The Basics of Supervisory Management: Mastering the Art of Effective Supervision*. New York: McGraw-Hill, 1975.

Blau, Peter M. & R. Schoenherr. *The Structure of Organizations*. New York: Basic Books, 1971.

Blau, Peter M. *Exchange and Power in Social Life*. New York: Wiley, 1964.

Borgmann, Albert. *Technology and Character of Contemporary Life: A Philosophical Inquiry*. Chicago: University of Chicago Press, 1984.

Boulding, Kenneth. *Human Betterment*. Beverly Hills: Sage Publications, 1985.

Burnham, David. *The Rise of the Computer State*. New York: Vintage Books, 1983.

Burnham, James. *The Managerial Revolution*. Bloomington, IN: Indiana University Press, 1960.

Callahan, R. E. *Education and the Cult of Efficiency*. Chicago: University of Chicago Press, 1962.

Campbell, Jeremy. *Grammatical Man: Information, Entropy, Language, and Life*. New York: Simon and Schuster, 1982.

Cherniss, Cary & Edward Egnatios. "Clinical Supervision in Community Mental Health." *Social Work Supervision: Classic Statements and Critical Issues*, ed. by Carlton E. Munson. New York: The Free Press, 1979.

"Code of Ethics of the National Association of Social Workers." Washington, DC: National Association of Social Workers, 1979.

Cyert, Richard. *The Management of the Non-Profit Organization*. Lexington, MA: D. C. Health, 1975.

Dalton, Gene W., Louis B. Barnes & Abraham Zaleznik. *The Distribution of Authority in Formal Organizations*. Boston, Graduate School of Business Administration, Division of Research, Harvard University, 1968.

Dornbusch, S. & W. R. Scott. *Evaluation and the Exercise of Authority*. San Francisco: Jossey-Bass, 1975.

Downs, Anthony. *Inside Bureaucracy*. Boston: Little, Brown, 1967.

Drucker, Peter F. *Managing for Results*. New York: Harper & Row, 1964.

Dreyfus, Hubert L. & Stuart E. Dreyfus. *Mind Over Machine: The Power of Human Intuition and Expertise in the Era of the Computer*. New York: The Free Press, 1986.

Durbin, Paul T. (ed.). *A Guide to the Culture of Science, Technology, and Medicine*. New York: The Free Press, 1984.

Easton, David. *A Systems Analysis of Political Life*. Chicago: University of Chicago Press, 1979.

Ellul, Jacques. *The Technological Society*. New York: Vintage Books, 1964.

Ellul, Jacques. *The Technological System*. New York: Continuum, 1980.

Emerson, R. M. "Exchange Theory, Part II: Exchange Relations, Exchange Networks, and Groups as Exchange Systems." *Sociological Theories in Progress*, ed. by J. Berger, M. Zelditch & B. Anderson. Vol. 2. Boston: Houghton Mifflin, 1972.

Epstein, Laura. "Is Autonomous Practice Possible?" *Social Work Supervision: Classic Statements and Critical Issues*, ed. by Carlton E. Munson. New York: The Free Press, 1979.

Etzioni, Amitai. *A Comparative Analysis of Complex Organizations*. New York: The Free Press, 1961.

Etzioni, Amitai. *A Comparative Analysis of Complex Organizations.* Rev. ed.; New York: The Free Press, 1975.

Etzioni, Amitai (ed.). *The Semi-Professions and Their Organization.* New York: The Free Press, 1969.

Etzioni-Haleoy, Eva. *Bureaucracy and Democracy: A Political Dilemma.* London: Routledge & Kegan Paul, 1983.

Florman, Samuel C. *Blaming Technology: The Irrational Search for Scapegoats.* New York: St. Martin's Press, 1981.

Florman, Samuel C. *The Existential Pleasures of Engineering.* New York: St. Martin's Press, 1976.

Forester, Tom (ed.). *The Microelectronics Revolution: The Complete Guide to the New Technology and Its Impact on Society.* Cambridge, MA: MIT Press, 1980.

Forrester, J. W. *Industrial Dynamics.* Cambridge, MA: MIT Press, 1961.

Frankena, William K. *Ethics.* 2nd ed.; Englewood Cliffs, NJ: Prentice-Hall, 1973.

Freidson, E. *Profession of Medicine.* New York: Dodd, Mead, 1970.

French, J. R. and B. H. Raven, "The Bases of Social Power." *Studies in Social Power,* ed. D. Cartwright. Ann Arbor: University of Michigan Press, 1959.

Friedrich, Carl J. "Some Observations on Weber's Analysis of Bureaucracy." *Reader in Bureaucracy,* ed. Robert K. Merton et al. Glencoe, IL: The Free Press, 1952.

Galbraith, John Kenneth. *The New Industrial State.* 4th ed.; Boston: Houghton Mifflin, 1985. Originally published 1967.

Garnson, W. A. "Power and Probability." *Perspective on Social Power,* ed. J. D. Tedeschi. Chicago: Aldine, 1974.

George, Claude S. *The History of Management Thought.* Englewood Cliffs, NJ: Prentice-Hall, 1972.

Gewirth, Alan. *Reason and Morality.* Chicago: University of Chicago Press, 1978.

Goodsell, Charles T. *The Case for Bureaucracy: A Public Administration Polemic.* Chatham, NJ: Chatham House, 1983.

Goss, M. "Patterns of Bureaucracy Among Hospital Staff Physicians." *The Hospital in Modern Society,* ed. E. Freidson. New York: The Free Press, 1963.

Greenwood, E. *The Practice of Science and the Science of Practice.* Papers in Social Welfare No. 1. Waltham, MA: Brandeis University, Florence Heller School for Advanced Studies in Social Welfare, 1960.

Gruber, Murray L., Richard K. Caputo and Thomas Meenaghan, "Information Management." In Felice Davidson Perlmutter (ed.), *Human Services at Risk: Administrative Strategies for Survival.* Lexington, MA: Lexington Books, 1984.

Gruber, Murray L. *Management Systems in the Human Services.* Philadelphia: Temple University Press, 1981.

Grusky, Oscar and George A. Miller (eds.). *The Sociology of Organizations.* 2nd ed.; New York: The Free Press, 1981.

Habernas, Jurgen. *Legitimation Crises.* Boston: Beacon Press, 1975.

Hage, J. *Communication and Organizational Control.* New York: Wiley, 1974.

Hage, Jerald. *Theories of Organizations: Form, Process, and Transformation.* New York: Wiley, 1980.

Haire, Mason (ed.). *Modern Organization Theory: A Symposium of the Foundation for Research on Human Behavior*. New York: Wiley, 1959.

Handy, Charles B. *Understanding Organizations*. 2nd ed.; New York: Penguin Books, 1981.

Hardy, Jean. *Values in Social Policy: Nine Contradictions*. London: Routledge & Kegan Paul, 1981.

Harrington, Michael. *The Politics at God's Funeral: The Spiritual Crisis of Western Civilization*. New York: Penguin Books, 1983.

Hasenfeld, Yeheskel. *Human Service Organizations*. Englewood Cliffs, NJ: Prentice-Hall, 1983.

Heilbroner, Robert L. *Between Capitalism and Socialism: Essays in Political Economics*. New York: Vintage Books, 1970.

Heilbroner, Robert L. *An Inquiry into the Human Prospect*. New York: W. W. Norton, 1974.

Herzlinger, Regina E. "Management Control Systems in Human Service Organizations." *Organization and the Human Services: Cross-Disciplinary Reflections*, ed. Herman D. Stein. Philadelphia: Temple University Press, 1981.

House, William C. (ed.). *The Impact of Information Technology on Management Operation*. New York: Auerbach, 1971.

Jacoby, Henry. *The Bureaucratization of the World*. Berkeley: University of California Press, 1973.

Johnson, T. *Professions and Power*. London: Macmillan, 1972.

Jonas, Hans. *The Imperative of Responsibility: In Search of an Ethics for the Technological Age*. Chicago: University of Chicago Press, 1984.

Kadushin, Alfred. *Supervision in Social Work*. New York: Columbia University Press, 1976.

Kahn, Alfred H. and Shiela B. Kamerman. *Helping America's Families*. Philadelphia: Temple University Press, 1982.

Kaplan, A. "Power in Perspective." *Power and Conflict in Organization*, ed. R. L. Kahn and E. Boulding. London: Tavistock, 1964.

Kahn, Robert L. et al. *Organizational Stress: Studies in Role Conflict and Ambiguity*. Reprint ed.; Malabar, Florida: Robert E. Krieger, 1981. Original edition, 1964.

Kaslow, Florence Whiteman, and Associates. *Supervision, Consultation, and Staff Training in the Helping Professions*. San Francisco: Jossey-Bass, 1977.

Keen, Peter G. W. and Michael S. Scott Morton. *Decision Support Systems: An Organizational Perspective*. Reading, MA: Addison-Wesley, 1978.

Kidder, Tracy. *The Soul of the New Machine*. New York: Avon Books, 1981.

Kutzik, Alfred J. "The Medical Field." In *Supervision, Consultation, and Staff Training in the Helping Professions*, ed. Florence Whiteman Kaslow and Associates. San Francisco: Jossey-Bass, 1977.

Lasch, Christopher. *Haven in a Heartless World: The Family Besieged*. New York: Basic Books, 1979.

Lasch, Christopher. *The Culture of Narcissism: American Life in an Age of Diminishing Expectations*. New York: Warner Books, 1979.

Leavitt, Harold J. "Applied Organization Change In Industry: Structural, Technical, And Human Approaches." *New Perspectives in Organization Research*, ed. W. W. Cooper, H. J. Leavitt, and M. W. Shelly. New York: Wiley, 1964.

Levy, Charles. *Guide to Ethical Decisions and Actions for Social Service Administrators: A Handbook for Managerial Personnel.* New York: Haworth Press, 1982.

Lipsky, Michael. *Street-Level Bureaucracy: Dilemmas of the Individual in Public Services.* New York: Russell Sage Foundation, 1980.

Lipton, D., R. Martinson and J. Wilks. *The Effectiveness of Correctional Treatment.* New York: Praeger, 1975.

Lowi, Theodore J. "The Political Impact of Information Technology." In Tom Forester (ed.), *The Microelectronics Revolution: The Complete Guide to the New Technology and Its Impact on Society.* Cambridge, MA: MIT Press, 1980.

Lyotard, Jean-Francois. *The Postmodern Condition: A Report on Knowledge.* Minneapolis: University of Minnesota Press, 1984.

McDermott, John. "Technology: The Opiate of the Intellectuals." In Albert H. Teich (ed.), *Technology and Man's Future.* 2nd ed.; New York: St. Martin's Press, 1977.

Meller, Yossef. "Structural Contingency Approach to Organizational Assessment of Social Service Organizations." Ph.D. dissertation, University of Illinois at Chicago, 1983.

Merton, Robert K., Aisla Gray, Barbara Hockey and Herman C. Selvin (eds.), *Reader in Bureaucracy.* Glencoe, IL: The Free Press, 1952.

Mesthene, Emmanuel G. *Technological Change: Its Impact on Man and Society.* Cambridge, MA: Harvard University Press; New York: New American Library, 1970).

Mesthene, Emmanuel G. "The Role of Technology in Society." In Albert H. Teich (ed.), *Technology and Man's Future.* 2nd ed.; New York: St. Martin's Press, 1977.

Micheles, Robert. *Political Parties: A Study of Oligarchical Tendencies in Modern Democracy.* New York: The Free Press, 1949.

Miller, I. "Supervision in Social Work." *Encyclopedia of Social Work.* New York: National Association of Social Workers, 1971.

Mills, C. Wright. *The Sociological Imagination.* New York: Oxford University Press, 1959.

Mitchum, Carl. "Philosophy of Technology." In Paul T. Durbin (ed.), *A Guide to the Culture of Science, Technology, and Medicine.* New York: The Free Press, 1984.

Montagu, Ashley and Floyd Matson. *The Dehumanization of Man.* New York: McGraw-Hill, 1983.

Mouzelis, Nicos P. *Organization and Bureaucracy: An Analysis of Modern Theories.* Chicago: Aldine, 1967.

Muller, Herbert J. *The Children of Frankenstein: A Primer on Modern Technology and Human Values.* Bloomington: Indiana University Press, 1970.

Mumford, Lewis. *Technics and Civilization.* New York: Harcourt Brace Jovanovich (A Harvest/HBJ Book), 1962. Originally published in 1934.

Munson, Carlton E. (ed.). *Social Work Supervision: Classic Statements and Critical Issues.* New York: The Free Press, 1979.

Meyers, Charles A. (ed.). *The Impact of Computers on Management.* Cambridge, MA: MIT Press, 1967.

Naisbett, John and Patricia Aburdene. *Re-inventing the Corporation: Transform-*

ing Your Job and Your Company for the New Information Society. New York: Warner Books, 1985.

Naisbett, John. *Megatrends*. New York: Warner Books, 1984.

Nutshell, G. and I. Snook. "Contemporary Models of Teaching." *Second Handbook of Research and Teaching*, ed. R. Travers. Chicago: Rand McNally, 1973.

Odiorne, George S. *Management by Objectives*. New York: Pictman, 1965.

Orlinsky, D. E. and K. I. Howard. "The Relation of Process to Outcomes in Psychotherapy." *Handbook of Psychotherapy and Behavior Change*, ed. S. Garfield and A. Bergin. 2nd ed.; New York: Wiley, 1978.

Orgega y Gassett, José. "Thoughts on Technology." In C. Mitchum and R. Mackey (ed.), *Philosophy and Technology*. New York: The Free Press, 1972. (First published in 1933.)

Orwell, George. *1984*. New York: Signet, 1949.

Parihar, Bageshwari. *Task-Centered Management in Human Services*. Springfield, IL: Charles C Thomas, 1984.

Parsons, Talcott. *Structure and Processes in Modern Societies*. Glencoe, IL: The Free Press, 1960.

Perlmutter, Felice Davidson and Simon Slavin. *Leadership in Social Administration: Perspectives for the 1980's*. Philadelphia: Temple University Press, 1980.

Perrow, Charles. *Complex Organizations: A Critical Essay*. 2nd ed.; New York: Random House, 1979.

Perrow, Charles. "Hospitals: Technology, Structure and Goals." *Handbook of Organizations*, ed. J. G. March. Chicago: Rand McNally, 1965.

Pettigrew, Andrew M. *The Politics of Organizational Decision-making*. London: Tavistock, 1973.

Prottas, J. M. *People-Processing*. Lexington, MA: D. C. Heath, 1979.

Rapoport, R. *Community as a Doctor*. London: Tavistock, 1960.

Raven, B. H. "A Comparative Analysis of Power and Power Preference." *Perspectives on Social Power*, ed. J. T. Tedeschi. Chicago: Aldine, 1974.

Raven, B. H. and A. W. Kruglanski, "Conflict and Power." *The Structure of Conflict*, ed. P. Swingle. New York: Academic Press, 1970.

Resnick, Hermand and Rino J. Pattie, *Change From Within: Humanizing Social Welfare Organizations*. Philadelphia: Temple University Press, 1980.

Rosenbaum, J. E. *Making Inequality*. New York: Wiley, 1976.

Roszak, Theodore. *The Cult of Information: The Folklore of Computers and the True Art of Thinking*. New York: Pantheon Books, 1986.

Roth, J. A. and E. Eddy. *Rehabilitation of the Unwanted*. New York: Atherton Press, 1967.

Ruzek, S. K. "Making Social Work Accountable." *The Professions and Their Prospects*, ed. E. Freidson. Beverly Hills, CA: Sage Publishers, 1973.

Sanders, D. H. *Computers in Business: An Introduction*. New York: McGraw-Hill, 1975.

Sarri, Rosemary C. and Yeheskel Hasenfeld (eds.). *The Management of Human Services*. New York: Columbia University Press, 1978.

Scott, W. Richard. "Professional Employees in a Bureaucratic Structure: Social Work." *The Semi-Professions and Their Organization*, ed. Amitai Etzioni. New York: The Free Press, 1969.

Simon, H. A. *Administrative Behavior*. 2nd ed.; New York: Macmillan, 1962.
Simon, H. A. "Authority." *Research in Industrial Human Relations*, ed. C. Arensberg. New York: Harper and Brothers, 1957.
Simon, H. A. *The New Science of Management Decisions*. New York: Harper & Row, 1960.
Simon, Herbert A. *The Sciences of the Artificial*. Cambridge, MA: MIT Press, 1969.
Simon, Yves. *A General Theory of Authority*. Notre Dame: Notre Dame University Press, 1980.
Slavin, Simon (ed.). *Social Administration: The Management of the Social Services*. New York: Haworth Press and the Council on Social Work Education, 1978.
Stanley, Manfred. *The Technological Conscience: Survival and Dignity in an Age of Expertise*. Chicago: University of Chicago Press, 1978.
Stein, Herman D. (ed.). *Organization and the Human Services*. Philadelphia: Temple University Press, 1981.
Stein, Herbert D. "The Concept of Human Service Organization: A Critique." *Organization and the Human Services: Cross-Disciplinary Reflections*, ed. Herbert D. Stein. Philadelphia: Temple University Press, 1981.
Stewart, Rosemary. *How Computers Affect Management*. New York: Macmillan, 1971.
Strauss, A., L. Schatzman, R. Bucher, D. Ehrlich and M. Sabskim. *Psychiatric Ideologies and Institutions*. New York: The Free Press, 1967.
Sullivan, Henry Stack. "Tensions, Interpersonal and International." *Tensions That Cause Wars*, ed. H. Cantril. Urbana: University of Illinois, 1950.
Taber, L. R. and R. H. Taber. "Social Casework." *The Field of Social Work*, ed. A. E. Fink. New York: Holt, Rinehart and Winston, 1978.
Tannenbaum, A. S. *Hierarchy in Organizations*. San Francisco: Jossey-Bass, 1974.
Taylor, Frederick W. *Scientific Management*. New York: Harper & Bros., 1911.
Teich, Albert H. (ed.). *Technology and Man's Future*. 2nd ed.; New York: St. Martin's Press, 1977.
Thompson, James D. *Organizations in Action: Social Science Bases of Administrative Theory*. New York: McGraw-Hill, 1967.
Thompson, Victor A. *Modern Organization*. New York: Alfred A. Knopf, 1961.
Toffler, Alvin. *Future Shock*. New York: Bantam Books, 1970.
Toffler, Alvin. *Previews and Premises*. New York: William Morrow, 1983.
Toffler, Alvin. *The Third Wave*. New York: Bantam Books, 1980.
Toren, Nina. *Social Work: The Case of a Semi-Profession*. Beverly Hills, CA: Sage Publications, 1972.
Tropman, John E. *Policy Management in the Human Services*. New York: Columbia University Press, 1984.
Twiss, Brian. *Managing Technological Innovation*. 2nd ed.; New York: Longman, 1980.
Ullman, L. P. *Institution and Outcome*. Oxford, England: Pergamon Press, 1967.
United Way of America. *Directory-Data Processing Activity*. Report of the Data Service Committee. Alexandria, VA: June, 1977.
Vergin, Roger C. "Computer-induced Organizational Changes." *The Impact of*

Information Technology on Management Technology, ed. William C. House. Princeton: Auerbach, 1971.

Weber, Max. *Basic Concepts in Sociology*, trans. H. P. Secher. Secaucus, NJ: Citadel, 1962.

Weber, Max. "Bureaucracy." *From Max Weber: Essays in Sociology*, trans. and ed. Hans H. Gerth and C. Wright Mills. New York: Oxford University Press, 1958.

Weber, Max. *Economy and Society*, Vols. I and II, ed. Guenther Roth and Claus Wittich. Berkeley, CA: University of California Press, 1978.

Weber, Max. *The Theory of Social and Economic Organization*, trans. A. M. Henderson and Talcott Parsons. New York: The Free Press, 1947.

Weinberg, Alvin. "Can Technology Replace Social Engineering?" *Bulletin of the Atomic Scientists*, 22 (December, 1966): 4-8. Reprinted in Albert H. Teich (ed.), *Technology and Man's Future*. 2nd ed.; New York: St. Martin's Press, 1977.

Weiner, Myron E. *Human Services Management: Analysis and Applications*. Homewood, IL: Dorsey Press, 1982.

Whisler, Thomas L. *Information Technology and Organizational Change*. Chicago: University of Chicago Press, 1973.

Whyte, William H. *The Organization Man*. New York: Simon and Schuster, 1956.

Wiener, Norbert. *Cybernetics: Or Control and Communication in the Animal and the Machine*. New York: John Wiley, 1948. 2nd ed.; Cambridge, MA: MIT Press, 1961.

Wiener, Norbert. *The Human Use of Human Beings*. New York: Avon Books, 1954.

Winner, Langdon. *Autonomous Technology: Techniques-out-of-Control as a Theme in Political Thought*. Cambridge, MA: MIT Press, 1977.

Winner, Langdon. *The Whale and the Reactor: A Search for Limits in an Age of High Technology*. Chicago: University of Chicago Press, 1986.

Yablonsky, Lewis. *Robopaths*. Indianapolis: Bobbs-Merrill, 1972.

Yates, Douglas. *Bureaucratic Democracy: The Search for Democracy and Efficiency in American Government*. Cambridge, MA: Harvard University, 1982.

ARTICLES

Abels, Paul. "Can Computers do Social Work?" *Social Work*, 17 (September, 1972): 5-11.

Administration in Social Work, 5 (Fall/Winter, 1981).

Aldrich, Howard. "Organizational Boundaries and Interorganizational Conflict." *Human Relations*, 24 (August, 1971): 279-93.

Anderson, Claire M. "Information Systems for Social Welfare: Educational Imperatives." *Journal of Education for Social Work*, 11 (Fall, 1975): 16-21.

Argyris, Chris. "The Organization: What Makes It Healthy?" *Harvard Business Review*, 36 (November-December, 1958): 107-16.

Auerbach, Isaac L. and Vladimir Slamecker. "Needed: Executive Awareness of

Information Resources." *Information and Management*, 2 (February, 1979): 3-6.

Bacharach, Samuel B. and Edward J. Lawler. "The Perception of Power." *Social Forces*, 55 (September, 1976): 123-34.

Bacharach, Samuel B. and Edward J. Lawler. "Power Tactics in Bargaining." Ithaca, NY: New York State School of Industrial and Labor Relations, Cornell University, 1980.

Bartezzaghi, E., C. Ciborra, A. DeMario, P. Maggiolini and P. Romano. "Computers, Management and Organization: Reflections on a Pilot Study." *Information and Management*, 4 (November, 1981): 239-58.

Bennis, Warren G. "Leadership Theory and Administrative Behavior: The Problem of Authority." *Administrative Science Quarterly*, 4 (September, 1959): 259-301.

Bierstedt, Robert. "An Analysis of Social Power." *American Sociological Review*, 15 (December, 1950): 730-38.

Blankenship, L. Vaughn and Raymond E. Miles. "Organizational Structure and Managerial Decision Behavior." *Administrative Science Quarterly*, 13 (June, 1969): 106-20.

Blau, Peter M. "Critical Remarks on Weber's Theory of Authority." *American Political Science Review*, 57 (June, 1963): 305-16.

Block, J. and J. Block. "An Interpersonal Experiment on Relations to Authority." *Human Relations*, 5 (No. 1, 1952): 91-98.

Brewer, John. "Flow of Communications, Expert Qualifications and Organizational Authority Structures." *American Sociological Review*, 36 (June, 1971): 475-84.

Boyd, Lawrence H., John H. Hylton and Steven V. Price. "Computers in Social Work Practice: A Review." *Social Work*, 23 (September, 1978): 368-71.

Caputo, Richard K. "The Role of Information Systems in Evaluation Research." *Administration in Social Work*, 10 (Spring, 1986): 67-77.

Cochran, Clarke E. "Authority and Community: The Contributions of Carl Friedrich, Yves R. Simon, and Michael Polanyi." *American Political Science Review*, 71 (June, 1977): 546-58.

Cohen, Michael D., James G. March and Johan P. Olsen. "A Garbage Can Model of Organizational Choice." *Administrative Science Quarterly*, 17 (March, 1972): 1-25.

Cohen, Neil A. and Gary B. Rhodes. "Social Work Supervision: A View Toward Leadership Style and Job Orientation in Education and Practice." *Administration in Social Work*, 1 (Fall, 1977): 281-91.

Coser, Rose Laub. "Authority and Decision-Making in a Hospital: A Comparative Analysis." *American Sociological Review*, 23 (February, 1958): 56-63.

Dahl, Robert A. "The Concept of Power." *Behavioral Science*, 2 (July, 1957): 201-18.

DeGrazia, Sebastian. "What Authority is Not." *American Political Science Review*, 53 (June, 1959): 321-31.

Delany, William. "The Development and Decline of Patrimonial and Bureaucratic Administrations. *Administrative Science Quarterly*, 7 (March, 1963): 458-501.

Dewar, Robert and Jerald Hage. "Size, Technology, Complexity and Structural Differentiation: Toward Theoretical Synthesis." *Administrative Science Quarterly*, 23 (March, 1978): 111-36.

Donahue, Jack H. et al. "The Social Service Information System." *Child Welfare*, 53 (April, 1974): 243-55.

Drezner, Stephen M. "The Emerging Art of Decision-Making." *Social Casework*, 54 (January, 1973): 3-12.

Drucker, Peter. "Managing the Public Service Institution." *Public Interest*, 33 (Fall, 1978): 43-60.

Ein-Dor, Philip and Eli Segev. "Information Systems: Emergence of a New Organizational Function." *Information and Management*, 5 (September-November, 1982): 279-86.

Ein-Dor, Philip and Eli Segev. "Organizational Context and the Success of Management Information Systems." *Management Science*, 24 (June, 1978): 1064-1077.

Emerson, R. M. "Power-Dependence Relations." *American Sociological Review*, 27 (February, 1962): 31-40.

Emgel, Gloria V. "Professional Autonomy and Bureaucratic Organization." *Administrative Science Quarterly*, 15 (March, 197): 12-21.

Etzioni, Amitai. "Authority Structure and Organizational Effectiveness." *Administrative Science Quarterly*, 4 (June, 1959): 43-67.

Fuller, Theron K. "Computer Utility in Social Work." *Social Casework*, 51 (December, 1970): 606-11.

Garvey, William D. and Belver C. Griffith. "Scientific Communication as a Social System," *Science*, 157 (September, 1967): 1,011-16.

Gibson, Cyrus F. and Richard L. Nolan. "Managing the Four Stages of EDP Growth." *Harvard Business Review*, 52 (January/ February, 1974): 76-88.

Gerth, H. H. and C. Wright Mills. "A Marx for the Managers." *Ethics*, 52 (January, 1942); 200-15.

Glisson, Charles A. and Patricia Yancey Martin. "Productivity and Efficiency in Human Service Organizations as Related to Structure, Size, and Age." *Academy of Management Journal*, 23 (March, 1980): 21-37.

Gruber, Murray. "Total Administration." *Social Work*, 19 (September, 1974): 625-36.

Grummer, Burton. "A Power-Politics Approach to Social Welfare Organizations." *Social Service Review*, 52 (September, 1958): 349-61.

Grummer, Burton. "Is the Social Worker in Public Welfare an Endangered Species?" *Public Welfare*, 37 (Fall, 1979): 12-21.

Hage, J. and M. Aiken. "Relationship of Centralization to Other Structural Properties." *Administrative Science Quarterly*, 12 (June, 1967): 72-91.

Hage, J. and M. Aiken. "Routine Technology, Social Structure, and Organizational Goals." *Administrative Science Quarterly*, 14 (September, 1969): 366-77.

Hage, Jerald. "An Axiomatic Theory of Organizations." *Administrative Science Quarterly*, 10 (December, 1965): 289-320.

Hall, R. H. "Professionalization and Bureaucratization." *American Sociological Review*, 33 (February, 1968): 94-104.

Harrison, Paul M. "Weber's Categories of Authority and Voluntary Associations." *American Sociological Review*, 25 (April, 1960): 232-37.

Hawkins, J. David., Rogver A. Roffman and Phillip Osborne. " 'Decision Makers' Judgments: The Influence of Role, Evaluative Criteria, and Information Access." *Evaluation Quarterly*, 2 (August, 1978): 435-54.

Hinings, C. R., D. J. Hickson, J. M. Penning and R. E. Schneck. "Structural Conditions of Intraorganizational Power." *Administrative Science Quarterly*, 19 (November, 1974): 22-44.

Holland, Thomas P. "Information and Decision Making in Human Services." *Administration in Mental Health*, 4 (Fall, 1976): 26-35.

Hoshino, George and Thomas P. Mcdonald. "Agencies in the Computer Age." *Social Work*, 20 (January, 1975): 10-14.

Hoshino, George. "Social Services: The Problem of Accountability." *Social Service Review*, 47 (September, 1973): 373-83.

Janowitz, Morris. "Changing Patterns of Organizational Authority: The Military Establishment." *Administrative Science Quarterly*, 3 (March, 1959): 473-93.

Kaplan, N. "The Role of the Research Administrator." *Science Quarterly*, 4 (June, 1952): 20-42.

Karl, Barry D. "Public Administration and American History: A Century of Professionalism." *Public Administration Review*, (September/October, 1976): 489-503.

Kline, Bennett E. and Norman H. Martin. "Freedom, Authority, and Decentralization." *Harvard Business Review*, 36 (May/June, 1958): 69-75.

Krieger, Leonard. "Authority." In *Dictionary of the History of Ideas*, ed. Philip P. Weiner. New York: Charles Scribner's Sons, 1973, vol. I, pp. 141-62.

Krieger, Leonard. "The Idea of Authority in the West." *American Historical Review*, 82 (April, 1977): 249-70.

Krocker, Donald W. "An Empirical Study of the Current State of Information Systems Evaluation." Doctoral dissertation, University of Georgia, Athens, 1976.

Leavitt, Harold J. and Thomas L. Whisler. "Management in the 1980's." *Harvard Business Review*, 36 (November-December, 1958): 41-48.

Lerner, B. and D. W. Fisk. "Client Attributes and the Eyes of the Beholder." *Journal of Consulting and Clinical Psychology*, 40 (1973): 272-77.

Levinson, Harry. "Management by Whose Objectives?" *Harvard Business Review*, 48 (July-August, 1970): 125-34.

Lewis, Harold. "Management in the Nonprofit Social Service Organization." *Child Welfare*, 54 (November, 1975): 615-23.

Lindblom, Charles E. "The Science of 'Muddling Through'." *Public Administration Review*, 19 (Spring, 1959): 79-88.

Lippott, R., N. Polansky and S. Rosen. "The Dynamics of Power." *Human Relations*, 5 (No. 1, 1952): 37-64.

Lorber, J. and R. Satow. "Creating a Company of Equals: Sources of Occupational Stratification in a Ghetto Community Mental Health Center." *Sociology of Work and Occupations*, 4 (August, 1977): 281-302.

McNeil, Kenneth. "Understanding Organizational Power: Building on the Weberian legacy." *Administrative Science Quarterly*, 23 (March, 1978): 65-90.

Mechanic, David. "Sources of Power in Lower Participants in Complex Organizations." *Administrative Science Quarterly*, 7 (December, 1962): 349-64.

Meyer, Marshall W. "Automation and Bureaucratic Structure." *American Journal of Sociology*, 74 (November, 1986): 256-64.

Meyer, Marshall W. "The Two Authority Structures of Bureaucratic Organization." *Administrative Science Quarterly*, 13 (September, 1968): 211-28.

Michels, Roberto. "Authority." *Encyclopedia of the Social Sciences*, Vol. II.

Moynihan, Tony. "Information Systems as Aids to Achieving Organizational Integration." *Information and Management*, 5 (September/November, 1982): 225-29.

Newman, Edward and Jerry Turem. "The Crisis of Accountability." *Social Work*, 19 (January, 1974): 5-16.

Nilson, L. B. "The Application of the Occupational 'Uncertainty Principle' to the Professions." *Social Problems*, 26 (June, 1979): 570-81.

Noble, John H. and Henry Wechsler. "Obstacles to Establishing Communitywide Information Systems in Health and Welfare." *Welfare in Review*, 8 (November-December, 1970): 18-26.

Noble, John H. "Protecting the Public's Privacy in Computerized Health and Welfare Information Systems." *Social Work*, 16 (January, 1971): 35-41.

Nurius, Paula S. and Elizabeth Mutschler. "Use of Computer-Assisted Information Processing in Social Work Practice." *Journal of Education for Social Work*, 20 (Winter, 1984): 83-94.

"On Power and Authority: An Exchange on Concepts." Communications. *American Sociological Review*, 25 (October, 1960): 731-32.

Parsons, Talcott. "Suggestions for a Sociological Approach to the Theory of Organizations." *Administrative Science Quarterly*, 1 (June, 1956): 63-85.

Parsons, Talcott. "Suggestions for a Sociological Approach to the Theory of Organizations." *Administrative Science Quarterly*, 1 (September, 1956): 225-36.

Patti, Rino J. and Michael J. Austin. "Socializing the Direct Service Practitioner in the Ways of Supervisory Management." *Administration in Social Work*, 1 (Fall, 1977): 267-80.

Perrow, Charles. "A Framework for the Comparative Analysis of Organizations." *American Sociological Review*, 32 (April, 1967): 194-208.

Peabody, Robert L. "Authority." *International Encyclopedia of the Social Sciences*, Vol. I.

Peabody, Robert L. "Perceptions of Organizational Authority: A Comparative Analysis." *Administrative Science Quarterly*, 6 (March, 1962): 463-82.

Pillsbury, Jolie Bain and Kathy Nance Newton. "An Evaluation Framework for Public Welfare Agencies." *Public Welfare*, 34 (Winter, 1976): 47-51.

Pondy, Louis R. "Organizational Conflict: Concepts and Models." *Administrative Science Quarterly*, 12 (September, 1967): 296-320.

Practice Digest, 6 (Winter, 1983).

Presthus, Robert V. "Authority in Organizations." *Public Administration Review*, 20 (Spring, 1960): 86-91.

Presthus, Robert V. "The Social Bases of Organization." *Social Forces*, 38 (December, 1959): 103-09.

Pugh, D. S., D. J. Hickson, C. R. Hinings, and C. Turner. "Dimensions of Organization Structure." *Administrative Science Quarterly*, 13 (June, 1968): 65-105.

Reif, W. E. and Robert M. Monczka. "Locating the Systems Department." *Journal of Systems Management*, 24 (December, 1973): 28-33.

Resnikoff, Howard L. "The Need for Research in Information Science." *Information and Management*, 2 (February, 1979): 1-2.

Rothschild, Ann M. and Jean E. Bedger. "A Regional CHILDATA System can Work: An Exchange of letters." *Child Welfare*, 53 (January, 1974): 51-57.

Schoech, Dick J. and Lawrence L. Schkade. "What Human Services Can Learn from Business About Computerization. *Public Welfare*, 38 (Summer, 1980): 18-27.

Scott, W. Richard. "Reactions to Supervision in a Heteronomous Professional Organization." *Administrative Science Quarterly*, 10 (June, 1965): 65-81.

Scott, Richard W., Sanford M. Dornbush, Bruce C. Busching and James D. Laing. "Organizational Evaluation and Authority." *Administrative Science Quarterly*, 12 (June, 1967): 93-117.

Sherman, Lawrence W. and Richard A. Berk. "The Specific Deterrent Effects of Arrest for Domestic Assault." *American Sociological Review*, 49 (April, 1984): 261-72.

Simon, Jules. "Authority." *Cyclopedia of Political Science, Political Economy, and of the Political History of the United States*, Vol. I.

Slavin, Simon (ed.). "Applying Computers in Social Service and Mental Health Agencies: A Guide to Selecting Equipment, Procedures and Strategies." *Administration in Social Work*, 5 (Fall/Winter, 1981).

Slonim, Jacob, Dave Schmidt and Paul Fisher. "Considerations for Determining the Degrees of Centralization or Decentralization in the Computing Environment." *Information and Management*, 2 (February, 1979): 15-29.

Smith, Clagett G. "A Comparative Analysis of Some Conditions and Consequences of Intra-Organizational Conflict." *Administrative Science Quarterly*, 10 (March, 1966): 504-29.

Smith, D. E. "Front-Line Organization of the State Mental Hospital." *Administrative Science Quarterly*, 10 (1965): 381-99.

Sterling, Theodore D. "Humanizing Computerized Information Systems." *Science*, 190 (December, 1975): 1,168-72.

Taylor, James C. "Some Effects of Technology in Organizational Change." *Human Relations*, 24 (April, 1971): 105-23.

Thomas, Edwin J., Claude L. Walter and Kevin O'Flaherty. "Computer-Assisted Assessment and Modification: Possibilities and Illustrative Data." *Social Service Review*, 48 (June, 1974): 170-83.

Thompson, Victor A. "Bureaucracy and Innovation." *Administrative Science Quarterly*, 10 (June, 1965): 1-20.

Thompson, Victor A. "Hierarchy, Specialization, and Organizational Conflict." *Administrative Science Quarterly*, 5 (March, 1961): 485-521.

Turem, Jerry S. "The Call for a Management Stance." *Social Work*, 19 (September, 1974): 615-23.

Udy, Stanely. "'Bureaucratic' Elements in Organizations: Some Research Findings." "Research Reports and Notes." *American Sociological Review*, 23 (August, 1958): 415-18.

Wasserman, Harry. "The Professional Social Worker in a Bureaucracy." *Social Work*, 16 (January, 1971): 89-95.

Weick, K. "Educational Organizations as Loosely Coupled Systems." *Administrative Science Quarterly*, 21 (March, 1976): 1-19.

Wright, Gordon R. "A System of Service Reporting: Its Development and Use." *Child Welfare*, 15 (March, 1972): 182-93.

Wrong, Denis H. "Some Problems in Defining Social Power." *American Journal of Sociology*, 76 (May, 1968): 673-81.

Young, David W. "Case Costing in Child Care: A Critical Step Toward Increased Accountability in Social Services." *Child Welfare*, 52 (May, 1973): 299-305.

Young, David W. "Management Information Systems in Child Care: An Agency Experience." *Child Welfare*, 53 (February, 1974): 102-11.

Zald, M. N. "Organizational Control Structures in Five Correctional Institutions." *American Journal of Sociology*, 68 (November, 1962): 335-45.

Zietz, G. "Hierarchical Authority and Decision Making in Professional Organizations." *Administration and Society*, 12 (November, 1980): 277-300.

Index